Choosing
Gratitude

Choosing Gratitude

YOUR JOURNEY TO JOY

Nancy Leigh DeMoss
with Lawrence Kimbrough

MOODY PUBLISHERS
CHICAGO

All Scripture quotations, unless otherwise indicated, are taken from *The Holy Bible, English Standard Version.* Copyright © 2000; 2001 by Crossway Bibles, a division of Good News Publishers. Used by permission. All rights reserved.

Scripture quotations marked NKJV are taken from the *New King James Version.* Copyright © 1982 by Thomas Nelson, Inc. Used by permission. All rights reserved.

Scripture quotations marked KJV are taken from the King James Version.

Scripture quotations marked NIV are taken from the *Holy Bible, New International Version®.* NIV®. Copyright © 1973, 1978, 1984 by International Bible Society. Used by permission of Zondervan. All rights reserved.

Emphasis in Scripture quotations is the author's.

All websites listed herein are accurate at the time of publication, but may change in the future or cease to exist. The listing of website references and resources does not imply publisher endorsement of the site's entire contents. Groups, corporations, and organizations are listed for informational purposes, and listing does not imply publisher endorsement of their activities.

Editor: Betsey Newenhuyse
Cover Design: The DesignWorks Group, Inc.
Interior Design: Smartt Guys design
Cover Image: Shutterstock/RF

Library of Congress Cataloging-in-Publication Data

DeMoss, Nancy Leigh.
  Choosing gratitude : your journey to joy / Nancy Leigh DeMoss with Lawrence Kimbrough.
    p. cm.
  Includes bibliographical references.
  ISBN 978-0-8024-3255-1
  1. Gratitude--Religious aspects--Christianity. I. Kimbrough, Lawrence, 1963- II. Title.
  BV4647.G8D46 2009
  241'.4--dc22
                            2009019693

Moody Publishers is committed to caring wisely for God's creation and uses recycled paper whenever possible. The paper in this book consists of 30 percent post-consumer waste.

We hope you enjoy this book from Moody Publishers. Our goal is to provide high-quality, thought-provoking books and products that connect truth to your real needs and challenges. For more information on other books and products written and produced from a biblical perspective, go to www.moodypublishers.com or write to:

Moody Publishers
820 N. LaSalle Boulevard
Chicago, IL 60610

3 5 7 9 10 8 6 4

Printed in the United States of America

Gratefulnesse

Thou that has given so much to me,
Give me one thing more—a grateful heart....

... I cry, and cry again;
And in no quiet canst Thou be,
Till I a thankful heart obtain
Of Thee.

Not thankful when it pleases me,
As if Thy blessings had spare days;
But such a heart, whose pulse may be
Thy praise.

GEORGE HERBERT (1593-1633)

With gratitude to

Byron Paulus, Executive Director of Life Action Ministries

One of the greatest joys of my life has been the blessing
of serving with you and Sue in the ministry of revival
for these past thirty years, as part of the Life Action team.

and

Greg Thornton, Vice-President and Publisher for Moody Publishers

What a privilege it has been to partner with you and the Moody team
over the past ten years, in the writing and release of (now) ten books.

You are two dear friends and fellow-servants.
I thank the Lord for your wise leadership and godly counsel
and for your prayers and encouragement,
all of which have helped me stay in the race and have
made me a more fruitful servant of Christ.

Only eternity will reveal all the hearts that have been revived
and the lives that have been transformed
as a result of your humble, faithful service for Christ.

Soli Deo Gloria

About the Author

Nancy Leigh DeMoss is the author of ten books including the bestselling *Lies Women Believe and the Truth That Sets Them Free* and *Choosing Forgiveness: Your Journey to Freedom*. She is the host and teacher for *Revive Our Hearts* and *Seeking Him*, two national syndicated programs heard each weekday on over 1,000 radio stations. Through her teaching ministry and books (which have sold more than 2,000,000 copies) God is using her as a mentor and spiritual mother to thousands of women—and has positioned her as a leader of the True Woman movement.

Nancy's burden is to call women to freedom, fullness, and fruitfulness in Christ and to see God ignite true revival in the hearts of His people. For more information on her radio programs, conference ministry, and books, visit www.ReviveOurHearts.com.

Contents

Before You
Begin

So many people do things *for* me or *to* me—as a quadriplegic in a wheelchair, someone has to help me out of bed, pour the coffee, get me dressed, brush my hair, brush my teeth, blow my nose . . . and I'm always quick to say, *"Thank* you." And I mean it.

What's more, I say it a lot. I remember when Judy, my executive assistant, came into my office and asked if she could borrow $10. I was busy, so I absentmindedly told her to take the bill out of my wallet, which she did. When I heard my purse snap shut, I automatically said in a cheery voice, "Thank you!" Immediately, a friend standing nearby said, "What did you thank *her* for? She's the one who ought to thank you." I guess I'm just programmed to express gratitude to people.

Oh, if it were only that way with the Lord Jesus. If only we were better "programmed" to be grateful—not only to people—but to Him, lifting appreciative prayers countless times during the day. Sadly, lack of gratitude—and often *ingratitude*—resides in our hearts. That's scary. Lack of a thankful spirit carries serious penalties—a quick read of Romans chapter 1 tells us that. And if a thankless spirit was the undoing of a generation eons ago, is it any different for us? In fact, you and I know God far better than those to whom He revealed Himself through mere creation–we have even *more* to be thankful for!

And so I've been giving thanks for most of my paralyzed life. Not only giving thanks *"in* everything," as one part of the Bible tells us, but "always giving thanks to God the Father *for* everything" as another part commands (1 Thessalonians 5:18; Ephesians 5:19-20 NIV). Most of us are able to thank God for His grace, comfort, and sustaining power *in* a trial, but we don't thank Him *for* the problem, just finding Him in it.

But many decades in a wheelchair have taught me to not segregate my Savior from the suffering He allows, as though a broken neck–or in your case, a broken ankle, heart, or home–merely "happens" and then God shows up after the fact to wrestle something good out of it. No, the God of the Bible is bigger than that. Much bigger.

And so is the capacity of your soul. Maybe this wheelchair felt like a horrible tragedy in the beginning, but I give God thanks *in* my wheelchair . . . I'm grateful *for* my quadriplegia. It's a bruising of a blessing. A gift wrapped in black. It's the shadowy companion that walks with me daily, pulling and pushing me into the arms of my Savior. And *that's* where the joy is.

My friend Nancy Leigh explains this so beautifully in her precious new book *Choosing Gratitude*. And it needs explaining! It's hard to hold on to gratitude; it's hard to find joy when you're looking into the jaws of mind-bending pain or heart-wrenching disappointment. But you have quite a guide in Nancy because she is ever so careful not to separate God from the suffering He allows in your life. She makes the connection between gratitude and joy.

Nancy leads you, step by step, through those select Scriptures and insights that are your journey into heaven-sent joy. Not a here-today-and-gone-tomorrow kind of gladness, but a deep and profound joy that simply cannot and will not be shaken. A joy that even sees you through those things you'd be quick to call tragedies.

In *Choosing Gratitude,* you'll discover that your affliction–that is, your "wheelchair," whatever it is–falls well within the overarching decrees of God. Your hardship and heartache come from His wise and kind hand and for that, you can be grateful. In it *and* for it. Finally, Nancy will reveal where the power to do that lies: We give thanks for everything *in the name of our Lord Jesus Christ.* Yes, it's her wonderful Savior that Nancy Leigh DeMoss is always careful to exalt. You'll discover that in this special book you hold in your hands.

Thank you, Nancy–and I mean that–*bless* you for not only instructing but modeling for us how living should be a litany of thanks to God . . . believe me, that kind of gratitude looks so very good on *you!*

Joni Eareckson Tada
Joni and Friends International Disability Center

Your Invitation to
Transformation

Could you, therefore, work miracles,
you could not do more for yourself than by this thankful spirit;
for it heals with a word speaking,
and turns all that it touches into happiness.

WILLIAM LAW[1]

For many months now, I have been looking carefully at what the Scripture has to say about the grace of gratitude. I've been meditating on what it means to be a grateful person, and why it matters.

This has not been merely an academic exercise for me. It has been so much more. The Lord has taken me on a personal journey—a journey I'm still very much on. He has shown me how vital it is to train my heart to respond to all of life with a thankful spirit, even in situations and seasons that I find unpleasant or difficult.

The trek hasn't always been an easy one—along the way He has shed light on things in my heart that were not pretty. His Spirit has brought conviction as my responses under pressure have been held up to the standard of how I've counseled and challenged others (not to speak of the standard of His Word!).

But this has been a good and needed process in my life, and the changes He is bringing about in my perspective and my character, along with the freedom that comes from saying, "Yes, Lord!" have more than compensated for the hard places. (I've shared more of this process in "A Personal PS," beginning on page 159.)

This book is an invitation to join me on that journey. I want you to see what I've seen. And I want you to experience the fresh joys I am encountering as I confront those stubborn weeds of ingratitude and choose to cultivate a thankful heart. Before we get started, however, I want to step back for a moment and reflect on where we're headed and why I believe it's so important for you to go there.

Prior to writing this book, if someone had asked me, "Are you a grateful person?" I would have scored myself "above average" on that front. And I think those who know me would generally agree.

Thanks, in large measure, to parents who insisted that the next order of business after receiving a gift was to write a thank-you note, the importance of expressing gratitude was impressed on me from my earliest years. It's just part of good manners, right? The polite thing to do. Though I didn't always appreciate it at the time, I'm grateful for that training today.

Over the years, I have sought to make gratitude a way of life. And I have experienced many of the blessings that accompany the "attitude of gratitude."

However, I've seen that if I am not ceaselessly vigilant about rejecting ingratitude and choosing gratitude, I all-too-easily get sucked into the undertow of life in a fallen world. I start focusing on what I don't have that I want, or what I want that I don't have. My life starts to feel hard, wearisome, and overwhelming.

At times, in the course of writing this book, I have allowed myself to get pulled back into that dangerous current. I have seen how a lack of gratitude manifests itself in fretting, complaining, and resenting–whether within the confines of my own thoughts or, worse yet, through venting those thoughts to others.

But in those moments when I have found myself gasping for air, feeling that I was going under, I've discovered that *gratitude truly is my life preserver*. Even in the most turbulent waters, choosing gratitude rescues me from myself and my runaway emotions. It buoys me on the grace of God and keeps me from drowning in what otherwise would be my natural bent toward doubt, negativity, discouragement, and anxiety.

Over time, choosing gratitude means choosing joy. But that choice doesn't come without effort and intentionality. It's a choice that requires constantly renewing my *mind* with the truth of God's Word, setting my *heart* to savor God and His gifts, and disciplining my *tongue* to speak words that reflect His goodness and grace–until a grateful spirit becomes my reflexive response to all of life.

A POWERFUL SECRET

In the pages that follow, I'm going to encourage you to choose gratitude, first and foremost because it is the only fitting response to a good and gracious God who has delivered us from our guilt.

But if from nothing more than self-interest, choosing gratitude makes sense.

To a significant degree, your emotional, mental, physical, and spiritual well-being, as well as the health and stability of your relationships with others, will be determined by your gratitude quotient.

Cultivating a thankful heart is a safeguard against becoming bitter, prickly, and sour. A grateful child of God can't help but be a joyful, peaceful, radiant person.

If you find discouragement, depression, fear, or anxiety among your frequent companions, you may tend to attribute them to difficult or painful circumstances that surround you. But I want to suggest that as challenging as your situation or your season of life may be, your frame of mind likely has less to do with your distressing circumstances than with your need to develop a thankful heart.

How else can you explain those believers around the world–spanning from ancient times to the present day–who scrape by with less than most of us can fathom, and whose days are perpetually beset with trials and tragedy, but who nonetheless manifest irrepressible peace and joy?

I was struck by a comment made by theologian and author Dr. Wayne Grudem in an online interview. When asked by C. J. Mahaney about areas where he was vulnerable to discouragement in ministry, Dr. Grudem responded, "Honestly, *I don't often become discouraged*. I continue to see evidence of God's work in my life and the lives of those around me, and *I am simply overwhelmed with thankfulness to Him*"[2] (italics added).

This is a timely word. In the midst of widespread home foreclosures, high unemployment, soaring national debt, and shrunken retirement accounts here in America, along with unending news of global unrest, starvation, and disease, it has become increasingly natural for people to become discouraged, even to feel, at times, as though God has abandoned this world. For those who love and follow Christ, the rising tide of secularism and moral relativism provides all the more temptation to become despondent.

I am convinced that we must cultivate the grace and spiritual discipline of gratitude if we are to avoid losing our footing in these days. An important key to not becoming overwhelmed by what is going on around us is looking for evidences of God's hand at work in the midst of the turmoil and being "simply overwhelmed with thankfulness to Him."

It is striking to me how many times in Scripture–particularly in the book of Psalms–we are exhorted to give thanks, to praise the Lord, to sing to the Lord. Even more so to realize how many of those passages were penned by someone in dire straits.

There is a reason for this constant biblical call to be thankful people. It points to a powerful secret, but one so few recognize, that it is overlooked in most anthologies I have seen on Christian virtues.

As we will see, gratitude is not merely a second-tier virtue in the Christian life–it is vital. And it is transformational. I truly believe a grateful spirit, rooted in the soil of God's goodness and grace, will radically impact how you view and respond to *everything* in your life.

So join me as we explore together this simple but profound trait called gratitude. I pray it will be for you a journey to greater freedom and joy–a journey closer to the heart of God.

CHAPTER ONE

The Power of
Gratitude

*Seek to cultivate a buoyant, joyous sense
of the crowded kindnesses of God in your daily life.*

ALEXANDER MACLAREN[1]

Thank you!

Those words were probably among the first you ever learned to say.

As I've been working on this book, a young family has been living in my home for an extended period, while working on their first home, a fixer-upper. Their little girl is currently seventeen months old and is just beginning to say words that are (almost) intelligible. (As she and I were "reading" a Winnie the Pooh book the other night, she said "Tigger" for the first time. It was quite the moment for "Aunt Nancy" and for her parents who witnessed the event.)

When Katelynn was less than a year old, her mom and dad started trying to train her to say "Please" and "Thank you." Although she can't quite say the words yet, she is getting the concept and has become quite proficient with the hand signals they've taught her to use to communicate "Please" and "Thanks."

In virtually every language, "thank you" is part of Vocabulary 101. Except for those who are hearing or verbally impaired, it's not difficult to vocalize. But there's a world of difference between being able to *say* "thank you"—and actually having a thankful heart.

Where does gratitude rank on your list of Christian virtues?

In an arsenal that's supposed to include things like mountain-moving faith, radical obedience, patient long-suffering, and second-mile self-denial, for many, *gratitude* feels like an optional add-on. Nice if you can get it, but not all that critical to making life run the way it should.

If in our mind there's an A, B, and C tier of Christian character traits, gratitude likely rattles down to one of those lower rungs—down there with hospitality and cheerfulness and going to church on Sunday night. Gratitude may appear on the deluxe models, but it's definitely not in the basic package—and not even in the same *category* as those other, more important pieces of heavy Christian machinery. We think.

And yet . . .

This issue of gratitude is far more significant than its lightweight reputation would suggest. What appears at first to be a cute little cameo to go with our finer things is in reality a much weightier, much more powerful, much more necessary component to our Christian life.

Try, for example, to sustain persevering faith—without gratitude—and your faith will eventually forget the whole point of its faithfulness, hardening into a practice of religion that's hollow and ineffective.

Try being a person who exudes and exhibits Christian love

–without gratitude–and over time your love will crash hard on the sharp rocks of disappointment and disillusionment.

Try being a person who sacrificially gives of yourself–without the offering being accompanied by gratitude–and you'll find every ounce of joy drained dry by a martyr complex.

As British pastor John Henry Jowett once said, "Every virtue divorced from thankfulness is maimed and limps along the spiritual road."

> True gratitude *is not an* incidental ingredient

True gratitude is not an incidental ingredient. Nor is it a stand-alone product, something that never actually intersects with life, safely denying reality out on its own little happy island somewhere. No, gratitude has a big job to do in us and in our hearts. And it is one of the chief ways that God infuses joy and resilience into the daily struggle of life.

WORSHIP OR WHINE

The importance of this matter of gratitude can hardly be overstated. I've come to believe that few things are more becoming in a child of God than a grateful spirit. By the same token, there is probably nothing that makes a person more *unattractive* than the absence of a grateful spirit.

I have learned that in every circumstance that comes my way, I can choose to respond in one of two ways:

I can *whine*

–or–

I can *worship!*

And I can't worship without giving thanks. It just isn't possible. When we choose the pathway of worship and giving thanks, especially in the midst of difficult circumstances, there is a fragrance, a radiance, that issues forth out of our lives to bless the Lord and others.

On the other hand, when we give in to whining, murmuring, and complaining, we end up on a destructive slide that ultimately leads to bitterness and broken relationships.

The consequences of an ungrateful spirit are not as readily seen as, say, those of a contagious disease. But they are no less deadly. Western civilization has fallen prey to an epidemic of ingratitude. Like a poisonous vapor, this subtle sin is polluting our lives, our homes, our churches, and our culture.

A grateful man or woman will be a breath of fresh air in a world contaminated by bitterness and discontentment. And the person whose gratitude is a byproduct of and a response to the redeeming grace of God will showcase the heart of the gospel in a way that is winsome and compelling.

So unless you just love the way duty feels when it wakes you up at three in the morning, or hijacks your plans for your day off, or hands you an unexpected bill that wasn't in the budget this month, don't try living the Christian life without gratitude. By sheer willpower and effort, you may succeed at "gutting out" right responses, but your Christianity (so-called) will be hollow, hard-edged, and uninviting to others.

THE POWER OF GRATITUDE

When real estate developer Peter Cummings first assumed his position as chairman of the Detroit Symphony Orchestra in 1998, he began writing personal thank-you notes to any donor who contributed $500 or more to the orchestra. He couldn't bear the thought of a symphony patron receiving a form letter with their name accidentally misspelled, or one of his friends being generically thanked above Peter's stamped signature.

Among the many notes that went out under his hand was one addressed to Mary Webber Parker, daughter of one of Detroit's leading families from an earlier generation, an heiress to the Hudson's department store fortune. She had moved away from Detroit nearly a lifetime ago, settled in California, and was now widowed, residing in an upscale nursing home outside of Hartford, Connecticut. And for some reason, she had decided to send a one-time check of $50,000 to her hometown symphony.

Peter's letter to Mary was, as usual, prompt and gracious . . . and unexpected. It must have thrilled the heart of this elderly widow (who had been back to Detroit only twice in the past twenty years) to hear of the orchestra's revitalization, made possible in part by her generous contribution.

Two weeks later, she wrote pledging another $50,000.

Within days, Peter had written her again, expressing his delighted gratitude and offering to come over from Michigan to visit with her sometime. He would be nearby when he took his daughter to register for college in Hartford the coming fall. He made no appeal for putting Mrs. Parker on the annual giving campaign–no "ask," as they say in fund-raising circles. Just a kind, personal attempt to say *thank you.*

Months passed. Then, in a letter dated June 13, Mary Webber Parker accepted Peter's request to come visit her in the fall. And if he wouldn't mind, she would like to give, not $50,000, but *$500,000* to the Detroit symphony.

Not once, but once a year–for five years.[2]

Two and a half million dollars!

Not out of duty. Not out of coercion. Not because she didn't have plenty of other suitors who would have bent over backwards to lure her as a benefactor.

She did it because someone was thankful. Genuinely thankful. That's the effervescent power of gratitude–the power to freshen the stale air of everyday life.

OUR HEART'S DESIRE

Still, it would surprise me to think that you woke up this morning saying, "My, if I could just be a more thankful person, my life would be so much better." Lack of gratitude rarely presents itself as a source of our problems.

Yet I *wouldn't* be surprised if you've been thinking to yourself lately, "I'm tired of my husband being so inconsiderate of me. I work nonstop to be sure his needs are met, and he gives me so little back in return. I wish just once he would stop and realize that there are other people besides him in this house who have needs."

Or perhaps, "I've given my parents every opportunity to apologize for putting me in a situation where I was abused as a child. A simple 'I'm sorry' would help. But all I ever get are excuses and rationalizations, always passing the blame onto someone else. I just want them to care. I want them to acknowledge how hard this has been to live with and how much it has cost me. Why can't they see that?"

Or, "Honestly, I'm not sure I even know what I believe anymore. I've lost all desire to pray, or read the Bible, or serve the Lord in any of the ways I used to. It just doesn't do it for me anymore. Going to church is a chore. All that spiritual zeal I used to have–people must have thought I was crazy. Maybe I was. I think everybody would be a whole lot better off if they just didn't let God get their hopes up."

I don't have to tell you that life hurts. If it's not one of these few examples I've given, it's a difficult child, a frustrating job, a serious (or perhaps just suspicious) medical issue, an in-law impasse. It could be a bad credit rating, a sleep problem, a lingering sin habit, maybe something as life-altering as a long, drawn-out divorce.

Big. Small. Long-term. Everyday. There are so many things about our individual life experiences that occupy our thoughts, feed our fears, and add to our worries. Whether we're out driving somewhere, or trying to sneak a nap, or attempting to pay attention to the pastor's sermon, all this "yuck" hangs on us like a spider web we can't seem to brush off.

We try everything we can think of to deal with it. We build our cases against the people who cause us the most grief in life. We seek out the supportive shoulders that are offered to let us air our complaints and annoyances.

Sometimes we sink into escape patterns, just trying not to think about it. We pour ourselves into our work in an attempt to avoid dealing with more important things.

But most likely, no matter how we try to cope with difficulty and disappointment, underneath it all is the heart's cry that keeps so many of us from experiencing God's best in our situations. With the promises of God still in force—even in the midst of aching pain and struggle—with His peace and presence still available to those who rely on Him, we too often choose to find our solace in these two plaintive words: "Why me?"

How often have you clung to this tart complaint, hoping to draw from it enough strength to protect your heart from further danger and damage?

"Why is life so hard?"

"Why can't other people just be normal?"

"Why did this have to happen to me?"

"Why won't anybody love me for who I am?"

"Why isn't God answering my prayers?"

"Why do I have to live alone like this?"

"Why doesn't the Bible work for me like it does them?"

"Why does this problem never seem to end?"

"Why am I supposed to just accept this?"

"Why me?"

Feeling betrayed. Feeling left out. Feeling inferior . . . mistreated . . . underappreciated. Like a whirlpool spinning around in never-ending circles, tugging and draining and pulling us down with every sweep of self-pity, we sink lower and lower into ourselves, into our problems.

Away from God.

Ungrateful.

"People tell me to keep my head up. They tell me this will only last for a season. But this 'season' of life has gone on for so long. And I still don't see any end in sight."

"You tell me to be thankful, Nancy. But you've never been in my shoes. If you had any idea what I've been through, you wouldn't be so quick to say that."

"I'm trying to accept what's happening, I'm learning to live with it. But gratitude? Are you saying I'm supposed to *like* being here?"

I promise you, dear friend, if all I had to share with you were some sweet platitudes about thankfulness, I wouldn't even try to respond to real-life statements like these. If all our faith had to offer were words that only fit in a church service or a theological textbook, it would be unkind of me to extend them to someone who is struggling to survive.

But true, Christ-centered, grace-motivated gratitude fits everywhere, even in life's most desperate moments and difficult situations. Even when there are no "answers," it gives hope. It transforms overwhelmed strugglers into triumphant conquerors.

THE GREATER PART OF GRATITUDE

The concept of gratitude is not entirely missing from our world. Just walk through a Hallmark store in the mall. You'll see lots of products on the shelves, decorated with daisies and pastel colors, encouraging us to think thankful thoughts. Their messages are inspiring, and I can appreciate the lightness and refreshment they offer in the midst of life's many challenges.

> Gratitude is a lifestyle. *A hard-fought,* grace-infused, *biblical lifestyle.*

But somehow, most of these expressions of gratitude seem more at home at a tea party than in the tumble and turmoil of a life that you and I know all too well.

You see, gratitude is a lot more than jonquils and journaling pages. Gratitude is a lifestyle. A hard-fought, grace-infused, biblical lifestyle. And though there's a sense in which anyone can be thankful—for God has extended His common grace to all—the true glory and the transforming power of gratitude are reserved for those who know and acknowledge the Giver of every good gift and who are recipients of His redeeming grace.

This book is about discovering what makes gratitude truly Christian. And how it makes life, even with all its bumps and bruises, a joy to behold.

* * *

The starting place for that discovery is coming to grips with two realities that at first blush seem to be anything but cause for thanks: human rebellion . . . and the execution of an innocent Man.

CHAPTER TWO

Guilt, Grace, and
Gratitude

*The thing that awakens the deepest well of gratitude
in a human being is that God has forgiven sin.*

OSWALD CHAMBERS[1]

It is one of the holiest moments any of us spend in the average week, month, or year—when we come to the table of the Lord to partake of the symbols of His body and His blood.

In this uniquely Christian ceremony, as we remember His death and celebrate our salvation, we are confronted again with the weight of our sin. It hangs in the stillness of the air around us, in the sacred silence that envelops our mind and emotions. For a few quiet moments, we are stripped of everything that normally distracts us from the things that matter most—no meetings to attend, no chores that need doing, no business to occupy our mind.

One by one, the elements rest in our hand as we wait for others to be served. There's nowhere to go, nowhere to hide. We are reminded that our very lives hang on the reality of what these items represent.

The sins of the past week–perhaps even the past few hours–parade into our thoughts. Things that seemed so justified, so compelling, so valid to us at the time now seem in this holy setting absolutely ridiculous. Shameful. "Why did we choose to act that way? How could we not have seen how foolish we were being? What were we thinking?"

But at some point in this process of repentance, when the weight of our fallenness becomes more than we can bear, hope reawakens in our soul. We are *not* impossibly saddled to these sins forever. In fact, they have already been forgiven! Jesus' grand statement–"It is finished"–applies to us, as well. Our position within His eternal kingdom is as sure as the Communion table, the trays, the loaf, the chalice, even the hands that serve its contents to us. By virtue of Christ's death and resurrection, we are free from sin, free to finally live, now and forever.

"Thank You, Lord!"

It is this very moment–this "thank you" moment–that sums up the whole objective of what we're doing here. The word "Eucharist" (the more liturgical term for what many of us call Communion or the Lord's Supper) comes to us from the Greek word *eucharistia*, meaning "the giving of thanks."[2] One Bible scholar explains it this way:

> Eucharist, which is also the word used for Holy Communion, embodies the highest act of thanksgiving for the greatest benefit received from God, the sacrifice of Jesus. It is the grateful acknowledgment of past mercies.[3]

So when we partake of Communion, we are engaged in gratitude. Gratitude to God. Gratitude for the gospel.

From guilt, through grace, to gratitude . . . all in one life-giving motion.

DO THE MATH

These three words–"guilt," "grace," and "gratitude"–are at the heart of the gospel. In a sense, they tell the story of the whole Bible.

We are born in a state of *inescapable guilt*, lawbreakers, under the just condemnation of a holy God, attempting (but unable) through human effort to make ourselves worthy and acceptable to God, good enough to earn His favor.

Into this hopeless situation comes the *undeserved grace* of God through Jesus Christ. Christ, who unlike us, perfectly fulfilled the law of God, died in our place as our perfect Substitute, taking the judgment we rightly deserved. His sacrifice on the cross means that we can stop trying to jump through spiritual hoops or manufacture our own righteousness (an impossible feat!). In that spectacular, extravagant gift of grace, everything we need for living in right relationship with our Creator has been provided.

Christ's life has become ours. His death has paid the sufficient sacrifice for our sins. His resurrection has assured us that not even the grave can keep God from fulfilling His promises. We are even now in forever fellowship with our heavenly Father.

It's the ultimate miracle. Certain death has been replaced by certain life. We who would never have sought after God on our own have been redeemed by One who sought *us* in His love and mercy. "For by grace you have been saved through faith. And this is not your own doing; it is the gift of God" (Ephesians 2:8).

That's the gospel–the good news! Our *guilt* has been swallowed up in the gift of God's *grace*–the only thing big and powerful enough to forever and fully overcome and remove that guilt.

What follows next, then, should be the logical reaction to this kind of rescue. Snatched from the brink of death, the burden of our sins lifted from our shoulders, you'd think the entire remainder of our earthly life wouldn't leave us adequate time for all the ways we'd want to say thanks. No longer dependent on our good works and performance, with the destination of our souls secured for all eternity, you'd expect that the energy of sheer gratitude, if nothing else, would propel us to never-ending acts of worship and service. "Whatever you want, Lord. It's the least I can do after all You've done for me."

If you'll bear with me for a brief Greek lesson (the language in which our New Testament was originally written), you'll see the connection between grace and gratitude even more clearly than we do in our English Bibles.

A moment ago, we saw that the word "eucharist" (Greek *eucharistia*) means the "giving of thanks." The root of that Greek word is *charis*, which is usually translated "grace." (The word for "gift"—*charisma*—is closely related.) But in numerous verses, that same word, *charis*, is translated "thanks."

Grace . . . gift . . . thanks (gratitude). The words are inseparable! And they should be inseparable in our hearts. Wherever you find *one*, you should expect to find the other.

All three—grace, gifts, and gratitude—are freely given. Our gracious, giving God generously and gladly bestows grace on recipients who deserve His judgment and wrath. Those who have received such an undeserved gift of grace, respond to the Giver in generous, glad gratitude.

Some of us cannot remember a time when we did not know these things. But have we lost the wonder of what it all means?

Note the way the apostle Paul did the mystifying math, "Where sin increased, grace abounded all the more" (Romans 5:20). Yes, in response to our abounding guilt, God poured out *super*-abounding grace. Should it not follow, then, that super-abounding grace ought to be met by *super-duper*-abounding gratitude?

But does it? Is the gratitude that flows out of your life as abounding as the grace that has flowed into your life?

Undeniable guilt, plus *undeserved grace*, should equal *unbridled gratitude*.

And yet, though we can readily affirm the biblical progression from guilt to grace, from death to life, from despair to hope, we find the next logical step a more difficult leap to make—not in theory,

> Is the gratitude that *flows out of your life* as abounding as the *grace that has flowed into your life?*

perhaps, but definitely in practice. For too many of us, responding to God's gift of grace with deep, profound gratitude is not something that shows up in our lives every day.

Why is that?

The rational argument is compelling. The thing we're after now is how to take what we know and make it what we live, how to make gratitude more than a perfunctory duty to be fulfilled.

I say we start by *making it our goal to have a heart that's as grateful toward God as the abounding grace He has poured into our life.*

That ought to keep us grateful for a long, long time. Grateful to God.

WHO'S TO THANK FOR THIS?

This is where Christian gratitude begins to rise above every other form of gratitude. Being humbly thankful to God for our salvation—the most undeserved transaction in our personal history—is the starting point for the purest form of gratitude: *God*-ward, *Christ*-

centered gratitude. True gratitude, Christian gratitude, doesn't exist in a vacuum; it has an Object.

Marvin Olasky, editor-in-chief of *World* magazine, recounts a conversation he had with a successful writer (and atheist) who mentioned how thankful he had felt during a recent vacation as he splashed in the ocean, absorbing the overwhelming beauty all around him, the settled feeling of being surrounded by the water's relaxing rhythms. Pressing him, Dr. Olasky asked whom the man was thanking. "Maybe the book buyers who had contributed to his affluence?" (Not that they created the ocean.) "Maybe his parents or his wife?" (Of course, they didn't make the ocean either.)[4]

The point is, true thankfulness requires a "you" to say "Thank you" to. And to be thankful to the living God implies a corresponding level of trust in Him that can only reside in a believer's heart.

To send up a "thank you" in heaven's general direction at the sudden appearance of a good parking spot, the dismissal of a speeding ticket, or a phone call from the doctor's office that tells you all your tests came back negative is not distinctively Christian gratitude. This kind of me-first thankfulness is the sort that only kicks in when things are going well and when positive blessings are flowing in our direction. It's little more than an automatic reflex, like saying "Excuse me" after accidentally bumping into someone, or "You too" after being encouraged by a salesclerk to have a nice day.

Christian gratitude, on the other hand, involves:

- *recognizing* the many benefits we've received from God and others (including those blessings that may come disguised as problems and difficulties),
- *acknowledging* God as the ultimate Giver of every good gift, and
- *expressing* appreciation to Him (and others) for those gifts.

Notice the difference between this concept of gratitude and other well-intentioned, upbeat, glass-half-full attempts at looking at life . . . looking on the bright side, choosing to dwell on whatever positives we can find in the midst of troubles and difficulties.

Certainly, there is everything right about striving to maintain a positive outlook on life–being grateful for one's health, for example, or for a chance visit with a friend in the grocery store aisle, or for a flower reaching full bloom in the garden, surprising you one morning as you step out the door on an otherwise gloomy day. How wonderful when our hearts awaken to the fact that we have so much to be thankful for!

But thankful to whom?

The problem with Christ-less gratitude is this: Nice as it is, it's out of context. It's a gratitude that generically tosses its thanksgivings into the air, not sure if they should be directed toward good luck, good breaks, good fortune, or the good Lord. Sensing the need to thank *someone* or *something* for making life not as bad as it might possibly be, people sincerely log these thoughts in a notebook or share them with friends, feeling good about feeling grateful.

These people have a vague awareness that they are part of something greater than mere human existence. Yet they are not ready–or not willing–to declare that this "something greater" is a personal Creator and Savior. Maybe a higher power, but not usually the God of the Bible, and certainly not the Lord Jesus Christ.

So while we can commend the practice of generalized gratitude, being glad to have friends and family members with a positive outlook on life, we cannot as believers be content to consider it sufficient for ourselves–not when there's a level of gratitude that offers us so much more than merely feeling good about how things are going.

Think of it this way. Why do we label the gifts we give to each other? Why do we seldom give something that's totally anonymous, where the other person has absolutely no idea who gave it to them? Why do we want them to know where this gift came from?

Is it because we're so vain that we can't stand the thought of not being recognized as the giver? Is it because we love feeling superior to others, consciously or subconsciously putting them in our debt?

Or is it simply because we want them to know that we value and appreciate them? "I want you to know how much you mean . . . to me."

So when the Bible declares that "every good gift and every perfect gift is from above, coming down from the Father of lights" (James 1:17), how can it be appropriate to thank our "lucky stars" for even a single blessing that comes our way, when in reality it has come from the One who thought up stars in the first place? The One who wants us to know that He has engraved us on the palms of His hands (Isaiah 49:16) and that He loves us "with an everlasting love" (Jeremiah 31:3).

Why would you want to miss that?

It is only by recognizing that our blessings have a single source—a real, personal, living, and loving Giver—that gratitude begins its transformation into authentic, *Christian* gratitude: *recognizing and expressing appreciation for the benefits we have received from God and others*.

ALL-AROUND GRATITUDE

Generic, garden-variety gratitude has its limits. Its scope is generally confined to certain terms and conditions—those that suit us or make us happy. It often doesn't look any higher than "eye" level, not caring so much about the state of others as being grateful we're not in the same shape ourselves. It also tends to be restricted to a mainly private experience, an internal thought process or discipline that largely only benefits us individually. And even though it sometimes does show itself in actively thanking others, it is usually less than full-bodied, whole-hearted gratitude, lacking the energy and eternal purpose of doing so in response to God's saving grace. It's just being grateful . . . because.

But the limits of *Christian gratitude*—

Who said anything about limits?

"Your steadfast love, O Lord, extends to the heavens, your faithfulness to the clouds. Your righteousness is like the mountains of God; your judgments are like the great deep" (Psalm 36:5-6)–His grace super-abounding from the far reaches of His dominion, filling the depths of our needy lives.

"The children of mankind take refuge in the shadow of your wings. They feast on the abundance of your house, and you give them drink from the river of your delights" (Psalm 36:7-8). Our hearts are answering back with all the gratitude we can muster, yet being met by (what's this?) even more grace and mercy.

Limits? *What* limits?

The beauty of Christian gratitude is that one little act of thanksgiving on our part–when directed toward or inspired by its rightful Recipient–can bound and rebound from one end of the kingdom to the other, not only blessing God, not only benefiting us, but even lodging itself in places and in people where God's love might never have been received any other way.

Want an example? Let's dive for a minute into the middle of 2 Corinthians, chapters 8 and 9. Fair warning, though: gratitude is going to be flying in all directions as we contemplate this passage. Don't be surprised if you get splashed a little.

Here's the background: Paul was reminding the brothers and sisters in Corinth about a collection he was taking up for the church in Jerusalem. Hard famine had left many people impoverished in the Jewish homeland. And Paul wanted to carry out the double task of providing humanitarian relief to his native people while also expressing the unity of the church–Gentiles sharing sacrificially with Jews, one in Christ.

The Corinthians (Gentiles) had promised at one time to do their part about pitching in. But as of the writing of this letter, they had not yet made good on their pledge, not the way others had–even those who possessed far fewer material resources than they did.

Paul was trying to get the Corinthians to see that by neglecting their *giving*, they were overlooking *grace* and stifling *gratitude*. If they would only let loose with an outpouring of grateful generosity, they would set off a wave of gratitude that would far exceed their sacrifice, sending thanksgiving up, down, and all around, rushing into areas where grace was needed the most.

Follow the bouncing ball of Paul's argument:

Grace begets giving. God has made "all grace abound to you, so that having all sufficiency in all things at all times, you may abound in every good work" (2 Corinthians 9:8). Since God has put such a huge supply of grace into our account, it's actually as though *He* is the one doing the giving through *us*. We give out of the abundance He has already given. (Talk about being part of something limitless–participating with God in dispersing His abundant blessings and saving grace throughout the whole world.)

But that's just the beginning.

Giving begets gratitude. By being "enriched in every way" and motivated toward generosity, our obedient hearts not only help meet others' physical or spiritual needs but also "produce thanksgiving to

God" through every person for whom our gifts are intended (v. 11). When we give out of gratitude to God, we cause gratitude to well up in others' hearts, as well.

As a result, gratitude begets even more gratitude. As recipients of grace, we have now become channels of this grace we've received, so that others may become the beneficiaries of His grace as well. The

> When we give out of gratitude to God, we cause gratitude to well up in others' hearts.

end result is that *even more* gratitude springs up–directed not just toward us but toward the Lord–their voices joining with ours in praise and appreciation. "For the ministry of this service is not only supplying the needs of the saints but is also overflowing in many thanksgivings to God" (v. 12).

How about that? Others are praising God because of our grace-induced gratitude and giving!

What has come down to us vertically has evoked heartfelt gratitude back to God. And out of His fullness, we have been inspired and enabled to shower gifts of grace horizontally in all directions, which in turn motivates even *more* thanksgiving to return vertically to God from *other* sources, thanks to what we've done (or more precisely, what God has done through us).

It's kind of like the rain cycle. Much the same way as water comes down from the sky, replenishing the earth, then returning to the air in evaporated moisture, Christian gratitude keeps God's grace churning full circle . . . and leaving who knows how many fruits and flowers and refreshed lives in its trail of glory.

HERE, THERE, EVERYWHERE

Be "abounding in thanksgiving," Paul encouraged the Colossians (Colossians 2:7). It's the picture of a river overflowing its banks during flood season, spilling out not in seeps and sprinkles but in gushing waves, scattering everywhere, leaving no section of ground untouched by the surging waters. Except *this* flood–this flood of gratitude–far from being a torrent of destruction, flows forth as a steady stream of blessing. Helping. Healing. Giving life.

Sound too airy and idealistic?

It isn't. I see it happening all the time among my coworkers in the ministry where I have served for more than thirty years. Most of the people God has called to this ministry raise part or all of their monthly financial support, as missionaries. These individuals and families are not out to see how much money they can make or how much stuff they can accumulate. To the contrary, many of them "survive" on an income that would be considered inadequate by today's standards.

And yet I can attest–just as Paul said of the Macedonian churches in 2 Corinthians 8:1–that these faithful servants excel in the grace of giving. As God provides (and He always does), they find delight in giving to one another, meeting each other's needs for everything from clothing to household items to fresh vegetables from the garden to practical assistance with auto and home repairs. (The "Blessing Barn," located in the ministry headquarters, does a brisk business!)

It's a beautiful thing to watch and be part of.

But even greater than seeing pantries stocked and closets supplied, is the joy of seeing relationships built, hearts knit together, and God glorified through His people in the process–all because of men and women who could easily choose hoarding and complaining, but instead choose giving and gratitude. To God and to others.

Grace, gratitude, and giving. They go hand in hand.

Try laying this same kind of spirit alongside situations in your own life, reaching out to the people you know and care about, encountering hurting places within your own church or extended family. Just think how many rifts and breaches could be mended, how many relationships restored and strengthened, if our gratitude for God's grace eclipsed our bitterness and overcame those relational barriers.

Imagine the impact in a world characterized by isolation, selfishness, and fractured relationships, if we were to adorn the gospel we profess to believe, with a culture of mutual care, concern, generosity, and sacrifice. The truth we proclaim would become believable. And God would be glorified.

That's what can happen every day of the week when God's grace becomes real in our lives, when we remember all that's been done for us through the miracle of redemption, when our first, heartfelt response is to say "Thank you"–both to God and to others–in whatever expression He wants it to take at the moment.

Abounding. Overflowing. Grace not only received and deposited, but daily withdrawn and multiplied.

That's what Christian gratitude will do.

* * *

So why don't we see more of this kind of robust, grace-based gratitude flourishing in our own hearts and among God's people? Among other reasons, there is a powerful challenger that counters true gratitude at every turn. And we don't have to look far to find that opponent; it lurks in every human heart.

CHAPTER THREE

No
Thanks

*Thankless children we all are, more or less, comprehending
but dimly the truth of God's fathomless love for us.*

ELISABETH ELLIOT[1]

It was nearly midnight on Friday, September 7, 1860, before the
Lady Elgin eased into the waters of Lake Michigan on its overnight
return trip from Chicago to Milwaukee. A passenger list of around
four hundred were on board, comprising mostly a Union militia
group and their families who had planned this late summer day-trip
as a fund-raiser for their unit.

The evening's activities had ended with dinner, dancing, and a
speech by Democratic presidential candidate Stephen A. Douglas.
And though the wind and spitting rain threatened ominous weather,
causing the captain to ponder delaying the voyage till morning, the
decision was finally made to heave anchor.

Spirits remained high among the partygoers long into the
night, as the spacious salons on board the *Lady Elgin* buzzed with

music and dancing. It was sometime between 2:00 and 2:30 in the morning, while the band was still playing, that a tremendous jarring shook the entire vessel, shattering the oil lamps and sending passengers into a darkened, rolling panic.

Augusta, a 130-foot schooner loaded with lumber and hurtling recklessly at full sail in the high wind, had struck *Lady Elgin*'s left rear side.

It should have been a somewhat glancing blow, the much smaller *Augusta* getting the worst of the accident. In fact, the crew of the steamer waved *Augusta* on, sure that the schooner was in greater need of haste toward the shoreline. But within a half hour, the boilers and engine had broken through the weakened bottom of the steamer, further rupturing the hull. The great ship was shivering off in pieces.

Lady Elgin was sinking.

For six hours, survivors floated on lifeboats and other bits of wreckage while lightning crackled across the sky, illuminating the horror. The northerly winds and furious surf drove the larger part of them backward toward a high bluff near Evanston, Illinois. Local residents and farmers, waking up to the sight of wailing men and women scattered across the water, ran for help, trying to organize a rescue party.

Among those recruited was Edward Spencer, a seminary student from nearby Northwestern University, who had grown up along the Mississippi River and knew how to handle himself in the water. Tying a long rope around his waist and diving into the choppy waters of western Lake Michigan, he pulled victim after victim to shore, struggling hard against the ferocious undertow that was claiming the last strength of many along the cliff walls, so tantalizingly close to safety.

While lunging and heaving with one person after another under his strong arm, the sharp edges of floating debris grazed his head and body. Again and again he returned to shore with another survivor, along with bloodied face and aching muscles.

But gathering strength and breath around a campfire, he would spot another person thrashing weakly in the surf. Tossing off the blanket that was conserving his body temperature, he hazarded out into the deeps again, muscles tensing and cramping as he strained against the current.

Eventually, of the thirty victims who survived along the water's edge in Evanston that day, seventeen of them would owe their lives to Edward Spencer's heroic efforts.

But although his bravery would be the beginning of new life for many, it became the end of a dream for the young seminarian. Never quite able to recover from the physical toll of that fateful day, he was forced to abandon his schooling, his livelihood, and his dreams of becoming a pastor and scholar. Some remember him being nearly paralyzed the rest of his life, often confined to a wheelchair.

And though his valor would at times be recalled in newspaper accounts and other general tributes, when asked by a reporter what he most recalled about the rescue, he replied, *"Only this: of the seventeen people I saved, not one of them ever thanked me."*[2]

Was that too much to expect?

LESSONS FROM A LEPER

Perhaps the most graphic illustration of ingratitude in the Bible is Jesus' healing of the ten lepers, found in Luke 17. You remember that these men who attracted Jesus' attention as He entered an unnamed village somewhere between Samaria and Galilee, "stood at a distance" as they called to Him (v. 12). They "lifted up their voices, saying, 'Jesus, Master, have mercy on us'" (v. 13).

So here, in the light of what we saw in the last chapter, we have a living picture of both *guilt* and *grace*, of human need and God's mercy.

Leprosy, you probably know, is symbolic of sin in Scripture—not that these men had sinned any more gravely than anyone else, but this infectious skin disease caused people to act and suffer in ways that illustrate the nature and consequences of sin. Being ceremonially defiled, for example, they were forced to live outside the village, separated from those who were able to walk around freely. In addition, the wasting evidence of leprosy on their limbs and facial features pictured the inward, often invisible scarring caused by sin's ravages on the human heart and spirit.

Therefore, when Jesus initiated their healing, sending them to the priests where the miraculous reversal of their condition could be officially and publicly certified, in the verses that follow, you would expect to see the third leg of our gospel trio.

Guilt encountered by *grace* should have issued forth in profound *gratitude*.

And yet, like those pulled to safety by Edward Spencer, gratitude remained hard to come by for the healed lepers. Some were probably (understandably) in a rush to get home to tell their family. Some were probably in a state of exuberant shock. Some perhaps went looking for Jesus later, but by that time had let the window for locating Him slip by.

You see, ingratitude is not always a calloused, who-cares shrugging of the shoulders. Sometimes it's just fourth or fifth on a list we never get around to following through on.

But for one of the healed lepers, gratitude was his *first*, immediate reaction to grace. Before running off at a dead sprint to do all the things he'd been missing during his years as an outcast, he returned from his appointment with the priest to say thanks to his Rescuer.

He didn't care who heard him. He didn't care how dusty the ground was at Jesus' feet. He didn't care where the others had gone or that he was there all by himself, his exuberant display making him look foolish to onlookers. All he wanted was to thank Him. Nothing mattered more. Before anything else, "Thank You, Lord!"

So when Jesus asked, "Were not ten cleansed? Where are the nine? Was no one found to return and give praise to God except this foreigner?" (vv. 17-18), the shame of ingratitude weighed heavily in the air, countered only by the loud, joyful words of one man's thanks, the fragrance of a grateful heart scenting the village streets.

Jesus' next words, directed to the grateful Samaritan, were even more precious than those that had originally brought about physical healing for the whole lot of outcasts: "Rise and go your way; your faith has made you well" (v. 19). Not just cured of his chronic physical condition, but secured with spiritual salvation.

The other nine returned to lives they thought they'd lost forever. They reunited with friends, with parents, with children. I'm sure they never forgot the day when their long, waking nightmare was miraculously transformed into a dream come true.

But unless they found their way to Jesus at a later time—in an event not recorded in the biblical accounts—they were left to enjoy their new life with at least this one caveat of emptiness: They may have come close to having everything restored to them, but they had not come close to Jesus.

THANKS FOR NOTHING

Ingratitude.

There is something especially distasteful and repulsive about this sin when we see it in others—especially when *we're* the ones whose generosity or sacrifice has gone unrecognized. Jesus, for example, had every reason to be annoyed at those who had received everything they ever wanted from Him, yet couldn't be bothered to say "thank you!"

And yet how often do we neglect to return thanks for a kindness done, a duty performed, or a step saved—while being oblivious to our ingratitude? Gradually, subtly, we become desensitized, as layers of entitlement and resentment wrap themselves around our hearts, until thankfulness is all but gone from our lives and lips.

> How often do we *neglect to return thanks* for a kindness done, *a duty performed, or* a step saved?

It isn't hard for it to happen . . . even in the most precious of relationships.

Many years ago, for example, I began giving a 30-day encouragement challenge to wives.[3] I encouraged them to confront ingratitude and cultivate a thankful spirit in their marriage with two simple steps:

1. For the next thirty days, purpose not to say anything negative about your husband—not to him, and not to anyone else about him.

2. Every day for the next thirty days, express at least one thing you admire or appreciate about your husband. Say it to him *and* to someone else about him.

It's amazing—and eye-opening—how difficult some wives have found this simple exercise to be.

One listener to our *Revive Our Hearts* broadcast said, "I made the commitment yesterday, but I've blown it already. I need mega-help. What attracted me to my husband of forty-two years was his quiet strength. But now, his being so quiet and easygoing drives me crazy." The hard work of holding back criticism and expressing gratitude proves to be almost impossible for some women.

Thankfully, many women have been willing to make the effort. Over the years, I've heard from hundreds of women who have taken this challenge. Many have been shocked to discover the extent of their ungrateful, critical spirit.

One woman wrote to say, "When I began this challenge, I thought I only spoke negatively to or about my husband once in a while. It was surprising to me how often thoughts came to my mind that I had to work at not letting pass through my lips. I've grown so accustomed to thinking a lot of bad things about him and then just blurting them out. This challenge has changed the way I communicate with my husband."

Ah, the difficult but rewarding walk from griping to gratitude!

Another wrote, "We've been married for forty years, and after listening to your message today, I realize that I have slowly let this practice of saying words of appreciation to my husband slip over the past few years. Starting today, I want to raise that level back up. As a matter of fact," she said, "he's out mowing the lawn as I'm writing this email, and as soon as he comes in, I'm going to compliment him on how nice the yard looks. It's a hot day and he's working so hard to make it look good."

It really is surprising how easily ingratitude can worm its way into our habit patterns.

But actually, it shouldn't be a surprise at all, because ingratitude is the taproot out of which grows a host of other sins. And if we don't put the axe to that root, we provide Satan with a wide, vacant lot on which to set up his little shop of horrors in our hearts.

Do you think I might be overstating the case a bit?

Well, when you think of the first chapter of Romans, what comes to mind? You may remember that in the opening paragraphs of this letter Paul talks about the "wrath of God" being revealed against the "unrighteousness of men" (v. 18). He lists "all manner of unrighteousness, evil, covetousness, malice" (v. 29), and a horde of other sins, including homosexual perversion and its acceptance and approval in a culture—just about every awful thing you can imagine.

But what is the beginning point of this vast array of vile activities? What starts people (and civilizations) down this path toward ever more serious sin? The answer is found in verse 21: "Although they knew God, they did not honor him as God *or give thanks to him,* but they became futile in their thinking, and their foolish hearts were darkened." That seemingly insignificant, innocuous matter of ingratitude turns out to be at the fountainhead of all the other evils listed in this chapter!

There's really no end to what can grow from the root of ingratitude. "An ungrateful person," Dr. D. James Kennedy pointed out regarding this passage in Romans, "is only one step away from getting his or her needs met in illegitimate ways."[4]

Do you see how serious this sin of ingratitude is? Remember how we talked in chapter 1 about the low rating some Christians place on gratitude, how it's often overlooked while we focus on "more essential" character traits? The fact is, when we give in to whining, murmuring, and complaining—not honoring God or giving thanks to Him (Romans 1:21)—we embark on a destructive slide that can take us down to depths we never could have imagined going.

Truly, ingratitude is our first step away from God.

INSTIGATORS OF INGRATITUDE

You may wonder if I'm making too much of this. But I assure you, this is not a light matter. Ingratitude is one of our enemy's most lethal weapons. Our homes and churches are suffering dreadfully from its effects. Our entire society, in fact, is feeling the fallout. So much of what is wrong in our lives–out of sync, out of sorts, out of harmony–can be traced back to this root of ingratitude. So we must guard our hearts against it at every turn, watching for the telltale signs, feelings, and attitudes that can set it off in us; things such as:

Unrealistic expectations. We can start to expect a lot–from life, from work, from others in general–until no matter what we're receiving in terms of blessing, it's never as much as we were hoping for. Needing God but not always wanting God, we expect *others* to take the place of God in our lives, depending on them to guide our decisions, to love us continuously and unconditionally, to provide for us emotionally, physically, socially, totally. And when they disappoint us–which inevitably happens–rather than being grateful for God's unchanging love and His faithfulness in meeting our needs, those unfulfilled expectations easily turn to resentment that poisons our hearts and relationships.

Forgetfulness. God warned the Israelites to be careful after they entered the Promised Land, not to forget the One who had rescued them from brutal slavery under the Egyptian taskmasters and had brought them into this good land. "Remember" is a key word in the book of Deuteronomy:

> "*Remember* that you were a slave in the land of Egypt, and the Lord your God brought you out from there with a mighty hand" (5:15).

"*Remember* what the Lord your God did to Pharaoh and to all Egypt" (7:18).

"*Remember* the whole way that the Lord your God has led you these forty years in the wilderness" (8:2).

"Beware lest you say in your heart, 'My power and the might of my hand have gotten me this wealth.' You shall *remember* the Lord your God, for it is he who gives you power to get wealth" (8:17–18).

But the children of Israel didn't remember . . . to the contrary, they *forgot*:

"You were unmindful of the Rock that bore you, and you *forgot* the God who gave you birth" (Deuteronomy 32:18).

"They *forgot* his works and the wonders that he had shown them" (Psalm 78:11).

"They *forgot* God, their Savior, who had done great things in Egypt" (Psalm 106:21).

Forgetfulness and ingratitude go hand in hand. They forgot to thank God for His deliverance, His faithfulness, His provision, His protection, and His miracles on their behalf.

We must *never forget* that "he has delivered us from the domain of darkness and transferred us to the kingdom of his beloved Son" (Colossians 1:13). We must *remember* that He has faithfully met our needs and sustained us by His grace.

To forget is not only to invite ingratitude but (as God told the ancient Hebrews in Deuteronomy 8:19) to "perish"—to watch a little of us die every day when we could be experiencing abundant life.

• *Entitlement.* I was interacting about this book with a friend in his eighties who has faithfully walked with and served the Lord for most of his life. In an email exchange he identified one of the most basic issues associated with ingratitude:

> In my own life I find that a default position, hidden beneath the surface, is an ever-present "entitlement" attitude. This, more than any other single thing I can identify, is my biggest problem.

When we take simple blessings for granted as if they were owed to us, or conversely, when we start to think that our house, our car, our wardrobe, or our general station in life is beneath what we deserve, ingratitude finds all the oxygen it needs to thrive.

> The higher our *standard of living, the* more discontented *we become.*

One of the unseemly side-effects of all the effort and energy our society has invested in building our individual and collective self-esteem is that our culture is now rife with this super-high level of deservedness. The more affluent we are, the higher our standard of living, it seems, the more demanding and discontented we become. Be careful where you place the bar for what you can and can't live with or without. The height of that baseline affects just about everything.

• *Comparison.* This is more than just keeping score on who has what and being perturbed because we don't have as much as they do. It is every bit as dangerous and deceptive for us to focus on the many sacrifices *we're* making, the hard work *we're* performing, the extra hours *we're* putting in, comparing our level of labor and commitment with what others are investing. Any time our focus is on ourselves–even if it's on the good things we're doing–it keeps us from being grateful for what others are contributing. We lose our appreciation for our spouse, children, friends, and coworkers when we constantly view them through our own shadow.

• *Blindness to God's grace.* We are the debtors. We are the ones who owe. The mercies of God that are "new every morning" (Lamentations 3:23) are not blessings we deserve but graces given by God's loving hand to fallen creatures, those whom He has redeemed by His good pleasure. To ignore such unmerited favor or consider it God's obligation to us is to miss out on the vision of His loveliness and glory that will sustain us through life's battles and keep joy flowing into and out of our heart.

Ingratitude steals it all–healthy relationships, humility, contentment, enjoyment, and the sweet walk with Christ that provides our only access to abundant life.

So there is good reason why in his second letter to Timothy, Paul listed ingratitude (ungratefulness) right in the middle of such evil companions as abusiveness, heartlessness, brutishness, and treachery (2 Timothy 3:1–5). Because that's where it belongs. Ingratitude is no less heinous a sin than these other evil traits.

In fact, so powerful is the influence exerted by ingratitude, that when we displace it with gratitude, we will likely find a multitude of other sins dislodged from our lives. Notice how Paul instructed the Ephesians: "Let there be no filthiness nor foolish talk nor crude joking, which are out of place, but instead *let there be thanksgiving"* (Ephesians 5:4).

When gratefulness returns, it brings with it the attending blessings and beauties of holiness.

And that's an expectation we can live with.

WHERE INGRATITUDE GOES TO DIE

Paul David Tripp, writing in *The Journal of Biblical Counseling*, recalled a scene he had witnessed more than once on his various travels to India. But this time, for some reason known only to the Holy Spirit, the Lord struck him with the gravity of it all at a deeper level than he'd ever experienced before.

Passing through New Delhi, in one of the most horrible slums in the world, he stood transfixed before a three-year-old boy leaning against the cot of his ailing, perhaps dying, mother. The boy's eyes were hollow, his stomach distended, his face fly-infested–the very picture of massive, helpless, noxious poverty.

The tears that streamed down Paul's cheeks in observing this tragedy were indeed the heartfelt evidence of his compassion. He longed to sweep this boy and his mother into his arms, away from these dreaded depths of sorrow and endless need.

But it was more than mere compassion he felt. It was an awareness that neither he nor this little boy had chosen their circumstances in life. The blessings of being raised among plenty, nurtured by godly parents, educated in quality schools, and given over to Christ at a young age began to roll over him in waves, even as he did his best to comfort and console the needy pair before him.

"You cannot explain the difference between that little boy and me by anything other than the Lord," he wrote. "Standing there in that slum, I felt all the complaints I had ever spoken as if they were a weight on my shoulders. I was filled with deeper gratitude than I think I have ever felt in my life."[5]

Not long after he arrived back home, Paul was visiting with a church leader from India who had come to the States to study. In the midst of their conversation, he asked the man what he thought of Americans, to which his guest responded—in polite, Asian style—"Do you want me to be honest?"

"Yes, I do," Paul answered.

But who could really be ready for this: *"You have no idea how much you have,"* the man said, *"and yet you always complain."*

We'd all have to agree, wouldn't we? At many levels, America can be rightly accused of gross ingratitude. But can the church and the Christians in America be accused of the same thing?

Can you? Can I?

Now would be a good time to speak to the Lord about it. If these words express your heart, join me in offering them up to Him:

Oh Lord, please forgive me for so often being forgetful of Your goodness, for acting as if I deserve anything more (or different) than what I have received, for sinfully comparing myself and my blessings with others', for being oblivious to so many expressions of Your grace, and for allowing roots of pride and ingratitude to grow up in my heart.

Forgive me for the many times and ways I reflect negatively on Your character and Your goodness, by verbalizing discontent and murmuring to others.

Grant me a spirit of true repentance and a heart that is always abounding, overflowing in gratitude toward You and others.

I'd expect He loves hearing that from us.

* * *

Left to ourselves, we do not naturally gravitate toward gratitude. What can motivate us to take our natural bent to the cross, to choose gratitude, and to allow the Spirit to make that the new default setting of our hearts? Thankfully, the Scripture offers all the motivation we need.

CHAPTER FOUR

Why Choose
Gratitude?

Gratitude unleashes the freedom to live content in the moment, rather than being anxious about the future or regretting the past.

ELLEN VAUGHN[1]

Matthew Henry, the eighteenth-century Puritan preacher whose Bible commentary remains among the most popular of all time, was once accosted by robbers while living in London.

Perhaps you've experienced this yourself–whether by having your car broken into or coming home to discover that your house had been burglarized. It's among the most unsettling things that can happen to a person. I'm sure it was, as well, for a quiet, thoughtful man of letters like Matthew Henry.

And yet, upon further reflection (as he wrote in his diary), he couldn't help but find something to be thankful for as a result of his misfortune:

Let me be thankful, first, because I was never robbed before; second, because although they took my purse, they did not take my life; third, because although they took my all, it was not much; and fourth, because it was I who was robbed, not I who robbed.[2]

What a perspective! As someone has said, "If you can't be thankful for what you receive, be thankful for what you escape."

It is simply true that the person who has chosen to make gratitude his or her mind-set and lifestyle can view anything–*anything!*– through the eyes of thankfulness. The whole world looks different when we do. And the one whose gratitude is Christian gratitude–directed not toward good genes or good timing but toward God Himself–finds that she deepens her relationship with Him on many levels.

We've established so far the fact that gratitude is the pure, appropriate response to the saving and keeping grace of God. We've also looked at its opposite–ingratitude–seeing how deceptively dangerous an ungrateful spirit can be in our lives and relationships.

But in the ongoing struggle of daily life–out there where feelings of disappointment and entitlement can easily talk louder than our best intentions–why choose gratitude over ingratitude?

For starters, here are eight good reasons. Personalizing and internalizing these alone, should be sufficient to continually outweigh whatever tempts us to whine when we should be worshiping.

1. GRATITUDE IS A MATTER OF OBEDIENCE

Oh, how I wish it was enough for you and for me to do something just because God has told us to–not because it would give us whiter teeth and fresher breath, or improve our debt-to-income ratio, or improve our dysfunctional relationships. No. Just because He says so.

Like being grateful, for instance.

"Offer to God a sacrifice of thanksgiving," the psalmist wrote, "and perform your vows to the Most High" (Psalm 50:14). "Oh give thanks to the Lord; call upon his name; make known his deeds among the peoples" (105:1). The Psalms are filled with exhortations to "thank the Lord for his steadfast love, for his wondrous works to the children of man" (107:8). The "attitude of gratitude" is a clear command and expectation of God.

This theme runs through the entire book of Colossians. In the course of just a few pages, the apostle exhorts believers about being "always" thankful (1:3), "abounding in thanksgiving" (2:7), devoting themselves to prayer, "being watchful in it with thanksgiving" (4:2). Then, as if summing up this whole idea, Paul seals it with one comprehensive, all-inclusive exclamation point: "Whatever you do, in word or deed, do everything in the name of the Lord Jesus, giving thanks to God the Father through him" (3:17).

If you're sitting down to dinner, be thankful.

If you're getting up to go to bed, be thankful.

If you're coming out from under a two-week cold and cough, if you're paying bills, if you're cleaning up after overnight company, if you're driving to work, if you're changing a lightbulb, if you're worshiping in a church service, if you're visiting a friend in the hospital, if you're picking up kids from school or practice . . .

Be thankful. God has commanded it—for our good and for His glory.

2. GRATITUDE DRAWS US CLOSE

God's command to be thankful is not the threatening demand of a tyrant. Rather, it is the invitation of a lifetime—the opportunity to draw near to Him at any moment of the day.

Do you sometimes long for a greater sense of God's nearness? When pressures intensify, when nighttime worries magnify in strength, when the days are simply piling up one after another, or when life simply feels dull and routine, do you crave the assurance of His presence?

The Scripture says that God inhabits the praises of His people (see Psalm 22:3 KJV). God lives in the place of praise. If we want to be where He is, we need to go to His address.

This is a recurring theme in the psalms: "Enter his gates with thanksgiving, and his courts with praise!" (Psalm 100:4). "Let us come into his presence with thanksgiving" (95:2). Thanks-giving ushers us into the very presence of God!

The tabernacle in the Old Testament was the place God set apart to meet with His people. In front of the entrance to the Holy of Holies–the sacred seat of God's manifest presence–stood the altar of incense, where every morning and every evening the priest would offer up the sweet scents, representing the prayers and thanksgiving of God's people who sought to draw near to Him.

Those ancient rituals were types and symbols of a relationship that we as New Testament believers can enjoy with God anytime, anyplace. Through His sacrifice on the cross, Christ has granted us access to the Father who dwells in us by His Spirit.

See what happens when you open your heart afresh to the Lord, moving beyond the normal, the canned, the almost obligatory phrases of praise and worship, where you truly begin to "magnify him with thanksgiving" (Psalm 69:30).

Yes, see if expressing gratitude to the Lord doesn't "magnify" Him in your eyes, increasing your depth perception of this One who knows your name, counts the hairs on your head, and manifests His love for you with one blessing after another. See if the practice of intentional gratitude doesn't transport you even nearer to Him—not just where your faith can believe it but where your heart can sense it. Thanksgiving puts us in God's living room. It paves the way to His presence.

3. GRATITUDE IS A SURE PATH TO PEACE

I know a lot of women who suffer from a noticeable deficiency of peace. I'm one *of* them sometimes. I'm not talking about a peace that equates to having a day with nothing on the calendar, plopping down on the sofa with a cup of hot tea and a good book. Not that this doesn't sound inviting, but let's be honest—that's a rare occasion for most of us. The peace

> Thanksgiving puts us in *God's living room.*

I'm talking about doesn't require a mountain cabin or a getaway weekend. It can happen anywhere, even in the most hectic moments and places of your life.

But only because gratitude knows where to look for it.

If we were sitting across the table from each other, you could tell me what's stealing your peace right now without having to think hard. You may be grieving a loss that never settles far from your conscious thoughts. You may be crying yourself to sleep at night over a situation with a son or daughter that is beyond your ability to control—a failing marriage, a little one undergoing diagnostic medical tests, perhaps open rebellion against God and against your parenting decisions. Maybe you're facing some health issues of your own, or your income just isn't meeting your monthly expenses, or your church is in turmoil over some hot-button issue.

We know that we can and should pray about these matters. But praying is not *all* that we can and should do. "Do not be anxious about anything," the apostle Paul wrote, "but in everything by prayer and supplication *with thanksgiving* let your requests be made known to God. And the *peace* of God, which surpasses all understanding, will guard your hearts and your minds in Christ Jesus" (Philippians 4:6–7).

To put it even more simply: In *every* situation . . . *prayer + thanksgiving = peace.*

When prayer teams up with gratitude, when we open our eyes wide enough to see God's mercies even in the midst of our pain, and when we exercise faith and give Him thanks even when we *can't* see those mercies, He meets us with His indescribable peace. It's a promise.

Oh, we can try it the other way. *Without* thanksgiving. Author and Bible teacher Beth Moore describes the way most people live, by substituting the familiar phrases from Philippians 4:6–7 with their polar opposites:

> Do not be calm about anything, but in everything, by dwelling on it constantly and feeling picked on by God, with thoughts like, "And this is the thanks I get," present your aggravations to everyone you know but Him. And the acid in your stomach, which transcends all milk products, will cause you an ulcer, and the doctor bills will cause you a heart attack, and you will lose your mind.[3]

Prayer is vital—but to really experience His peace, we must come to Him with gratitude. Hard gratitude. Costly gratitude. The kind that trusts that He is working for our good even in unpleasant circumstances . . . the kind that garrisons our troubled hearts and minds with His unexplainable peace.

Are you facing one or more chaotic, unsettled situations? Is your soul weary from striving, stress, and strain? There is peace, my friend—God's peace—waiting for you just beyond the doors of deliberate gratitude. But the only way to find it is to go there and see for yourself. God's peace is one of the many blessings that live on the other side of gratitude.

4. GRATITUDE IS A GAUGE OF THE HEART

When you ask some friends over for dinner, it's a sure sign that you enjoy their company and are comfortable spending time with them. When you choose church over sleeping in on Sundays, it suggests that you value worship and Christian fellowship more than political roundtables, leisurely brunches, or the *New York Times* crossword puzzle.

And when you catch yourself being grateful to God for His obvious and even His more subtle (or hard to understand) forms of blessing, it's an indication that your heart is being drawn to His, and that you believe He is good, faithful, and can be trusted.

If you start sensing godly gratitude welling up throughout the course of the day, it won't be because you're working hard to keep a New Year's resolution. Not for long. The only people who can sustain a consistent flow of thanksgiving between them and God are those who know who, what, and where they'd be if He hadn't intervened and saved them from themselves.

"Surely the *righteous* shall give thanks to your name," the psalmist wrote (Psalm 140:13). Giving of thanks is an indicator of our true heart condition. Those who have been made righteous by the grace of God will be thankful people.

Several years ago, I had the privilege of interviewing Joni Eareckson Tada, my dear friend who has lived her entire adult life as a quadriplegic, the result of a diving accident at the age of seventeen. For more than forty years, Joni has inspired countless others—myself included—with her joyful resilience in the face of extreme physical limitations and numerous other legitimate causes for whining and complaining.

What Joni didn't know the day we sat down to visit, was that my heart was weighed down with some ministry burdens that felt overwhelming at the time. Truth be told, it had been months since I had experienced or exhibited unfettered joy. As we talked, I was captivated by the indomitable spirit and joy of this woman who has a myriad of challenges and problems that make my own seem minuscule. Wanting counsel for my own heart as much as for our radio listeners, I asked Joni, "How do you maintain such a joyful spirit, with all the challenges you're forced to deal with on a daily basis?"

With just the slightest pause, she said, "You know, Nancy, I think I've just disciplined myself for so many years to 'give thanks in all things,' that it's become my reflex reaction."

The grateful heart that springs forth in joy is not acquired in a moment; it is the fruit of a thousand choices.

Of all the insights Joni shared that day, that single statement penetrated my heart the most deeply. I realized that for years, more often than not, my reflexive reaction to difficult circumstances had been to "whine," rather than giving thanks *from the outset*. That reaction of fretting, giving in to discouragement, and expressing negative thoughts about pressures and problems, had become my default pattern. That day, the Lord showed me my need to develop a new pattern of responding, one of "giving thanks in all things." I can't say that I'm there yet, but that is where I want to live.

The grateful heart that springs forth in joy is not acquired in a moment; it is the fruit of a thousand choices. It is a godly habit and pattern that over time becomes a new muscle in our spiritual makeup. And though like every other sanctified character trait, it does nothing to make us more loved and accepted by God, gratitude does become a reliable measure for where our hearts are with Him. Look for it, listen for it–and you'll learn a lot about how you're growing–or deficient–in grace.

5. GRATITUDE *IS* THE WILL OF GOD

I hear from a lot of people who want to know how to know the will of God for their lives, especially when it comes to major, life-ordering decisions. We all find ourselves at times needing and seeking His guidance, on matters as big and potentially confusing as college, career, and marriage choices.

But interestingly, when you go to the Scripture for insight on the will of God, you don't find a lot about things to do, places to go, or people to meet. That's because God's will is not so much a place, a job, or a specific mate, as it is a *heart* and a *lifestyle*. What you do find in the Word, however, are a few clear statements in regard to what the will of God is–not just for you, not just for me, but for all of us.

And one of them is gratitude. "Give thanks in all circumstances; for this is the will of God in Christ Jesus for you" (1 Thessalonians 5:18).

Sure, details matter to God. The specifics of what church to attend, what house to write a contract on, what position to apply for, and maybe even what hotel to stay at on vacation, are decisions He gives us wisdom to make, as we seek Him and walk in line with the principles of His Word.

But live long enough, and you find that the choices only change by year and color. A decision that's huge today usually shrinks in hindsight, replaced by yet another batch of options that fit whatever stage of life we're currently in. That's when you discover that the will of God is a whole lot bigger and broader than fine-print details and exact measurements. Instead, it's characterized by a handful of simple constants that overshadow our specific questions and our appeals for direction.

In other words, you may find yourself a lot closer to hearing God's heart on a certain time-sensitive matter, not by making pro- and con- lists or anguishing between multiple options, but simply by doing what you already *know* *t*o be His will.

"Give thanks in all circumstances; for *this is the will of God* in Christ Jesus for you." When faced with perplexing circumstances, when you don't know what to do or which way to go, be grateful—and you'll find yourself right in the middle of His will.

6. GRATITUDE IS AN EVIDENCE OF BEING FILLED WITH THE SPIRIT

"What does it mean to be filled with the Holy Spirit?" "How can we know that we are filled with the Spirit?" Those questions have generated a spate of books, broadcasts, and banter among preachers, theologians, and Christian authors. The answers vary, depending on the theological system being reflected. Some emphasize certain "spectacular" evidences of being filled with the Spirit. Others believe certain of those evidences ceased with the completion of the biblical canon.

However, on one point we can all agree: that believers—both individually and collectively—are to be filled with the Spirit of God. And the one passage in Scripture that explicitly commands us to "be filled with the Spirit" (Ephesians 5:18) describes for us what a Spirit-filled individual or body of believers "looks like"—the visible evidences of this invisible reality. We see that the Spirit-filled life has practical ramifications in every sphere in which we live and operate.

Some of the evidences that accompany, validate, and result from the filling of the Spirit are:

- Mutual edification with Scripture-based words and singing (5:19)
- Worship of God from the heart (5:19)
- Humility and mutual submission (5:21)
- Godly family structures and relationships (5:22-6:4)
- Appropriate attitudes and behavior in the workplace (6:5-9)
- Victory in spiritual warfare (6:10-18)

The one evidence I bypassed in the list above is no less important than all these others. It's found in Ephesians 5:20: "Giving thanks always and for everything to God the Father in the name of our Lord Jesus Christ." Being thankful is a prime evidence of being filled with the Spirit!

We would not for a moment believe that a man who abuses his wife is a Spirit-filled Christian. Nor would we believe a woman who claims to be filled with the Spirit, while embezzling funds from her boss.

No more, then, can we believe that a person who habitually gripes, murmurs, and worries about his pressures and problems, rather than "giving thanks always and for everything," is filled with the Spirit!

The fact is, we cannot whine and complain and be filled with the Spirit at the same time. When a thankful spirit resides in our hearts and expresses itself on our lips, it's an evidence that the Holy Spirit lives in us, that we are yielding to His control, and that He is producing His gracious fruit in and through our lives.

7. GRATITUDE REFLECTS JESUS' HEART

One of those qualities of the Lord Jesus that you may overlook if you're not observant is His spirit of gratitude. It's noticeable on several occasions:

• *At the return of the seventy disciples.* Jesus had dispatched these followers into the various cities and towns of the surrounding region, instructing them to proclaim the kingdom of God everywhere they went. As they returned home to report what had occurred through their ministry, they were almost too excited to get the words out. To see the joy of Christian service painted across their faces and decorated by their excited words caused Jesus to step back and marvel at the way the Father works through His people: "*I thank You*, Father, Lord of heaven and earth, that you have hidden these things from the wise and understanding and revealed them to little children; yes, Father, for such was your gracious will" (Luke 10:21). To watch Jesus, almost seeming awed Himself at the work of the Trinity, of which He (of course) is a part, is enough to make me want to gaze at God's work from my lowly vantage point and be amazed more often. More thankful.

• *At the tomb of Lazarus.* Even before making the official pronouncement for Lazarus to "come forth," Jesus turned to His Father–pre-answer–and said, "*I thank you* that you have heard me" (John 11:41). It's not hard to thank God *after* He answers our prayers and we've seen the desired outcome. The test of faith and surrender to the will of God is the ability to express thanks *before* we know how He will respond.

• *At mealtime.* If your pre-meal blessings are anything like mine, they are too often little more than thoughtless pauses before diving into what is set before you. Not for Jesus. I can only imagine that the blessing He said as He "looked up to heaven" and broke the loaves to distribute to the five thousand was one of deep, personal praise and thanksgiving. (In the Mark 8 account of His feeding of the *four* thousand, the writer states that Jesus prayed before handing out the bread, and again before handing out the fish–a blessing before each course!)

• *When facing suffering.* In my mind, the most remarkable instance we have of Jesus giving thanks took place at the Last Supper. Within hours of His betrayal, arrest, and trial, to be followed shortly by His crucifixion, Jesus observed the Passover feast with His disciples. The Jewish ceremony involved not just one, but multiple cups of "the fruit of the vine." When you combine and harmonize the Gospel accounts, it appears that Jesus paused at least three times during the Passover observance to *give thanks*:

- during supper, before taking the cup (Luke 22:17)
- before distributing the bread (Luke 22:19), and
- after supper, before taking another cup (Matthew 26:27)

Heightening the significance of what some might consider an inconsequential detail, all three of the Synoptic Gospels, as well as the apostle Paul, note the fact that Jesus *gave thanks* before partaking of the elements (Matthew 26:27; Mark 14:23; Luke 22:17–19; 1 Corinthians 11:24). He understood that these emblems represented His body and blood, soon to be broken and poured out in horrific fashion for the salvation of sinful man.

On a night when from a human perspective He had every reason to be self-absorbed and to give in to self-pity, resentment, or murmuring, He spoke words of *thanks* to His heavenly Father, words that flowed out of a thankful heart.

> Jesus gave Himself
> *to God and to the world,*
> not under coercion,
> *but* with gratitude.

That is no small deal. This was not just an obligatory blessing offered up before a meal. The whole meal pictured the enormous sacrifice Jesus was about to make. In giving thanks for the cup and the bread, then in giving the symbolic elements to His disciples, Jesus was saying in effect, "Yes, Father, I willingly surrender Myself to Your calling for My life, whatever the cost." He gave Himself to God and to the world, not under coercion, but with abandon and . . . *with gratitude*, grateful for the privilege of obeying His Father and of fulfilling the mission He had been sent to earth to complete.

My own heart is convicted as I write these words and I think how often my service for the Lord and others is tinged with shades of reservation (measured, "thus far but no further") and resentment over the price to be paid. *Oh Father, forgive me for my thankless sacrifices and service. May the thank-full Spirit of Christ fill and overflow my heart as I seek to fulfill Your calling for my life.*

8. GRATITUDE GETS US READY FOR HEAVEN

It's what we'll be doing forever. Oh, I'm sure it's not *all* we'll be doing forever, and yet I am confident that every action, thought, word, or undertaking throughout our entire, endless life with the Lord will be an expression of (literally) undying gratitude.

We know that day and night, the four living creatures in heaven "never cease to say, 'Holy, holy, holy, is the Lord God Almighty, who was and is and is to come!'" (Revelation 4:8). The twenty-four elders fall on their faces before Him, saying, "*We give thanks to you*, Lord God Almighty, who is and who was, for you have taken your great power and begun to reign" (11:17). Even now. Right this minute. Gratitude is the unending anthem of heaven.

And every time we speak and live out our thankfulness here on this very temporary base of operations, we join our voices with the grand chorus of gratitude that wells up before the throne of God, and we prepare ourselves for what we'll be doing throughout all eternity, glorifying and thanking Him for all He is and all He has done.

So think of today as a "dress rehearsal." And do it just the way you will when you're doing it "live" at the actual performance.

* * *

Eight reasons—and so many more—to be thankful people. Some choose gratitude. Most do not. Either way, the implications of that choice are further reaching than we can possibly imagine.

CHAPTER FIVE

Of Whiners and
Worshipers

*One thing is indisputable: the chronic mood of looking
longingly at what we have not, or thankfully at what we have,
realizes two very different types of character.*

LUCY C. SMITH[1]

In our attempts to better understand both ourselves and each
other, we commonly lump people into one of two mutually exclusive
categories, descriptions that nearly require a person to be either one
or the other.

Givers and takers.

Lovers and fighters.

Type As and Type Bs.

Free spirits and list makers.

Some of these traits seem to be inborn; others are more the
result of choices we make in life. But depending on which side that
we either find ourselves or place ourselves, the result is a whole
different set of outlooks and actions from those who operate out of
the other camp.

Two kinds of people. Optimists and pessimists. Early risers and night owls. Yankee fans and Red Sox fans. Grateful people and ungrateful people. Those who whine and those who worship. You can hardly be both. Maybe in spots, maybe in seasons. But throughout the balance of your life, one or the other will dominate the way you view and respond to most everything. You will choose to either be thankful or unthankful, to recognize a blessing or to overlook it, to acknowledge a kindness or to mindlessly ignore it.

You decide.

The old-time hymn writer Fanny Crosby had that choice to make. I'm sure when she learned that her sightless world was the result of a doctor's foolish mistake, she was forced to deal with wondering "what might have been." The hot compresses her physician had employed to cure her eye infection at six weeks of age had only succeeded in scarring sensitive tissue. His act had rendered her permanently blind.

Few of us know what it's like not to see—not being able to describe the color yellow, or distinguish a loved one's face in the crowd, or navigate a city block or street crossing simply by spotting obstacles and watching the traffic. What if even the simplest tasks of pouring your breakfast cereal, or counting change, or sorting the laundry required the intently focused attention of your hearing and touch? We forget to be thankful for the blessing of sight.

Yet Fanny Crosby, writer of more than eight thousand hymns, enough to fill fifteen complete hymnals stacked one on top of the other, enough to cause her publishers to resort to ascribing to her multiple pen names to make her output seem more believable, saw things another way.

She was *thankful* for the blessing of blindness.

At eight years of age, she composed this bit of verse, a poem not all that mature in grammar perhaps, but likely more mature than some of us ever become, even in old age:

Oh, what a happy child I am, although I cannot see,
I am resolved that in this world contented I will be,
How many blessings I enjoy that other people don't,
So weep or sigh because I'm blind, I cannot–nor I won't.

Imagine being able to say, as Fanny Crosby did, "I could not have written thousands of hymns if I had been hindered by the distractions of seeing all the interesting and beautiful objects that would have been presented to my notice." As she wrote in her autobiography, "It seemed intended by the blessed providence of God that I should be blind all my life, and *I thank Him* for the dispensation" (italics added).

"I thank Him." For blindness.

Two kinds of people: the grateful and the ungrateful. It's the difference between squandering life and sharing life, between being blinded to glory and "To God Be the Glory," between assured bitterness and "Blessed Assurance."

It's a difference you can see.

As I've already said–but can't help repeating–we pay an incalculable price for our ingratitude. After decades of ministry to hurting people, I have come to believe that a failure to give thanks is at the heart of much, if not most, of the sense of gloom, despair, and despondency that is so pervasive even among believers today. I believe many of the sins that are plaguing and devastating our society can be traced back to that persistent root of unthankfulness that often goes undetected.

This "attitude of gratitude" is something that desperately needs to be cultivated in our hearts and homes. Its presence—as we saw in the last chapter—brings a host of other blessings in its train, but its absence has profound repercussions.

I want to paint two contrasting portraits in this chapter—highlighting six differences between grateful people and ungrateful people. As you read each point, stand back and take a look at both pictures and then ask: Which most closely resembles my life? Do I have the marks of a worshiper or a whiner?

BETTER THAN I DESERVE

A grateful person is a humble person, while ingratitude reveals a proud heart.

When a friend tells you something she's thankful for, she's revealing a lot more than just the way she feels about a specific person or circumstance. She may tell you how thankful she is for her family, or for the relief of being spared from a certain danger, or for the peaceful place she finds herself in at the moment. But a person who's consistently grateful—and quick to express it—is actually telling you a lot more than that.

That's because gratitude is a revealer of the heart, not just a reporter of details. And among the things it reveals about us most is our level of humility.

I can still hear my dad answering that everyday question—"How are you doing?"—with a response that went far beyond the usual "Oh, just fine." When asked how he was doing, he would often say, "Better than I deserve." What prompted that response? The answer is that Art DeMoss never got over the fact that God had saved him, and that if he'd really gotten what he legitimately had coming to him, he would have been over his head in heartache.

My dad was quite the rebel as a young man, recklessly involved in gambling and troublemaking. But on October 13, 1950–a date he often rehearsed as he would share the story with others–God opened his eyes, showed him Christ Jesus, and brought him to repentance and faith. I rarely, if ever, recall him telling that story without tears in his eyes.

That's because he understood who he was and where he'd come from. He knew where God had found him and where he might well have ended up if God had not intervened in his life. That's the kind of person who doesn't have to go to great lengths to explain who he is or parade his accomplishments. His gratitude does all his explaining for him. "A humble mind," Henry Ward Beecher once said, "is the soil out of which thanks naturally grow."

But when a person feels entitled to his blessings, as though he's owed a job and a paycheck, a happy home and a healthy body, a sporty car and a spiffy retirement, you don't have to ask a lot of "How are you doing?" questions to know who you're dealing with. A visible lack of gratitude fills in all the blanks, and his responses to most anything reveal a proud heart.

Reminds me of the story of two old friends who happened upon each other at the store one day. One of the men was obviously in a foul, depressed mood, not even able to work up a weak smile to celebrate this chance encounter with a face and voice from his past.

"What's the trouble, buddy?" the other man asked.

"Oh, let me tell you, my uncle died three weeks ago and left me $40,000."

"Really?"

"Yeah, then the week after that, a cousin I hardly even knew died and left me $85,000. Then last week, one of my great-aunts passed away and left me a quarter of a million dollars."

"You've got to be kidding me?" his friend exclaimed. "Then why the long face?"

"This week . . . *nothing!*"

So that story is no doubt fictitious! But every hint of ingratitude —even when it's not so blatant—is an indicator of pride in our hearts. Henry Ward Beecher was right when he observed, "A proud man is seldom a grateful man, for he never thinks he gets as much as he deserves."

Pride is the father of ingratitude and the silent killer of gratitude. We think we deserve so much. But what does any of us have that we haven't received? What does any of us possess that doesn't come down from the One "who richly provides us with everything to enjoy" (1 Timothy 6:17)?

MAKING IT PERSONAL: *Do you more often manifest a humble, grateful spirit, or a proud, self-sufficient, ungrateful heart?*

I ONLY HAVE EYES FOR YOU

A grateful heart is God-centered and others-conscious, while an ungrateful person is self-centered and self-conscious.

In 1973, when the Presbyterian Church in America was just forming, the fledgling denomination had only two missionaries. One of them, a man named Dick Dye, was laboring hard in the Mexican mission field of Acapulco, with little to show for his efforts, and little money to keep him there much longer. The strain was starting to wear on him, as day after day he struggled with the endless demands, the toll on his body, soul, and spirit, and an uncertain future. He had every reason to question God's purpose for having him there—and every reason to moan about it to anyone who would listen to him.

But Dick Dye was not the kind of man to keep his head down. And on occasion when his gaze would lift toward the mountains surrounding Acapulco, he could see at a distance—high above the city—a huge cross visible from just about everywhere. For a God-centered man who knew there was more to his missionary work than measurable results and positive prayer-letter statistics, the sight of that cross was what kept him going some days. Remembering who he was serving, remembering why he was there, remembering to be grateful even with so much to be dismayed about—he was enabled to put one foot in front of the other, praising God as he plodded on month after month.

One day, Dick decided to drive up into the mountains to see if he could locate this massive cross, see if he could get a better look at it. When he finally got there, he found that the cross was affixed to a large hotel.

And found again that it's hard for God-centered people to keep from being others-centered, as well.

Wheeling into the parking lot and walking up to the front desk, Dick asked to speak to the manager. "Do you have an appointment?" the receptionist asked.

"No, ma'am, I just want to tell him something."

"What do you want to tell him?"

"Uh, well, I just . . . want to tell him 'thank you.'"

When Dick was finally received into the manager's office, when he told him how inspirational and encouraging the cross on this hotel had been to him while lonely and discouraged down in the city, the man lowered his head to his desk and began to sob.

After several awkward minutes, when at last he was able to compose himself, he whispered through choking tears, "That cross has been up there for years, and all I've ever heard about it is criticism.

You're the first person who's ever come to me and said, 'Thank you for having that cross there.'"

"Well," Dick said, trying to explain his natural inclination for being drawn to it, "see, I'm a missionary in the city, so . . ."

"Where does your church meet?" the man interrupted.

"Actually, we don't meet anywhere. I mean . . . we don't have a place to meet."

"Come with me," the manager said, walking him toward a beautiful chapel on the hotel property. Standing inside, he said to Dick, "We have church here at 9:00 a.m. and 11:00 a.m. every Sunday. But from now on, at 10:00 a.m., it's yours. You can begin services here next week."

Within a matter of years—from this surprising beginning—God raised up four Mexican congregations under the oversight of Presbyterian missionary Dick Dye. And it all started with a simple thank you—and with two men who were both as God-centered as they were others-centered.[2]

Grateful people are loving people who seek to bless others, while ungrateful people are bent on gratifying themselves. They tend to focus on "my needs," "my hurts," "my feelings," "my desires," "how I have been treated, neglected, failed, or wounded." An unthankful person is full of himself, seldom pausing to consider the needs and feelings of others.

Incidentally, I believe this is why a common end result of ingratitude is the sin of moral impurity. A person who is wrapped up in herself, whose whole world revolves around getting her own needs met, is prime bait for a tempter who thrives on accusing God of being unfair and ungenerous. An ungrateful heart is quick to notice when self is feeling unsatisfied, and is vulnerable to resorting to sinful acts and behaviors in an attempt to eliminate pain and experience personal pleasure.

MAKING IT PERSONAL: *Do you tend to be more focused on your own needs and feelings or on blessing and serving God and meeting the needs of others?*

I'M FULL, THANK YOU

A grateful heart is a full heart, while an unthankful heart is an empty one.

"By any measure of affluence," Chuck Colson has said, "the average American enjoys a quality of life beyond anyone's wildest dreams even a few decades ago."[3] Among the statistics he reports, citing Gregg Easterbrook's *The Progress Paradox: How Life Gets Better While People Feel Worse:*

- Real per-capita income has doubled since 1960.
- Life expectancy has nearly doubled in the past century and continues to rise.
- The size of the average new home in America has grown from 1,100 square feet (post–World War II) to 2,300 today.
- The average Westerner is more prosperous than 99.4 percent of everyone who's ever lived on earth.

> *Even during the lowest troughs of the recent economic downturn, Americans are still blessed beyond what most of the world can fathom.*

Even during the lowest troughs of the recent economic downturn, Americans are still blessed beyond what most of the world can fathom.

And yet in spite of such affluence, the percentage of Americans who describe themselves as "happy" is no higher today than in the

1950s. And the number of us who suffer from bouts of depression is listed conservatively in the 25 percent range.

In contrast to our penchant to be sad in the midst of plenty, think of the apostle Paul who, from the bowels of a Roman dungeon, deprived of all but the most basic necessities of life, wrote in a thank-you note, "I have all, and abound; I am full" (Philippians 4:18 KJV). His friends had largely abandoned him. His enemies were numerous. Whatever creature comforts he had enjoyed at one time were far away and probably destroyed. He was stripped bare of everything except mere existence, and yet . . . full.

What would your note from prison have sounded like? Or mine?

The difference between being full and empty is not usually between being rich or poor, at home or away, cupboards bursting at the seams or thinly lined with soup cans and Ramen noodles. The difference is gratitude.

Ungrateful people are much like a container that has a hole in it, leaking out every blessing that's been poured in, always needing something else, something new to consume for satisfaction fuel.

They are like the children of Israel from distant centuries past, whom Moses warned, "Take care . . . lest, when you have eaten and are full and have built good houses and live in them, and when your herds and flocks multiply and your silver and gold is multiplied and all that you have is multiplied, then your heart be lifted up, *and you forget the Lord your God*" (Deuteronomy 8:11–14).

Full, but never full enough.

Steve Dale, a syndicated columnist who answers people's questions about their pets, received an email from someone seeking advice on what to do with her twelve-year-old boxer that had a large tumor on his leg. Two different veterinarians had agreed that the tumor needed to be removed, but admitted that doing so would require the loss of the dog's leg. "Any advice?" the letter writer asked.

Dale responded that three-legged dogs actually seem to adjust fairly quickly after surgery, and are soon getting around just about as well as before, fetching balls and terrorizing squirrels. "The psychological trauma of being expected to feel sad because they've lost a limb just doesn't seem to occur. Instead, quite the reverse, they act overjoyed to be alive."[4]

Oh, to be more like Paul . . . and like a three-legged dog. To have a full heart even when deprived of creature comforts, rather than an empty heart while surrounded with (but oblivious to) abundant blessings. Gratitude is often the only difference between pervasive sadness and pure satisfaction.

> **MAKING IT PERSONAL:** *Are you more prone to focus on what you wish you had (or didn't have) or on the blessings you do have that are far greater than you deserve? Do you have a full heart, or does your heart "leak out" the blessings God pours in, always needing something more to be satisfied?*

FINE WITH ME

People with grateful hearts are easily contented, while ungrateful people are subject to bitterness and discontent.

David Brainerd was sick and unhealthy for most of his young, tuberculosis-shortened life. Not exactly the kind of condition with which to brave the wilds of the wintry Northeast, enduring blizzards, starvation, and long days of want to minister all by himself to the Native Americans of western Massachusetts in the mid-1700s.

One time, after falling ill once again in his little hut, he wrote in his now-famous journals, "Blessed be the Lord that I am not exposed in the open air. I have a house and many of the comforts of life to support me." On another occasion, having faced long weeks of solitude, "forging through swamps on rocky terrain through dark nights and cut off from all human companionship," he wrote, "*What reason for thankfulness I have* on account of this retirement"[5] (italics added).

> Ungrateful people *tend to hold tightly* to their rights.

Contact with people was nice, he said, but being alone with God drew him into intimacy with his Savior. He could choose to be thankful for that.

Yes, grateful people are easily contented, while the ungrateful easily become prisoners to bitterness.

I have spoken with many women who are chronically unhappy, "down," or depressed. The details and reasons vary, of course. But I have become increasingly convinced, after lots of these kinds of conversations, that one of the chief reasons behind a pervasive sense of blues and blahness is a failure to be thankful.

Ungrateful people tend to hold tightly to their rights. And when others fail to perform the way they want or expect them to, they feel justified in making demands and retaliating emotionally.

It's the opposite of what we see in the life of Ruth in the Old Testament who, having lost home and husband and finding herself alone with a cantankerous mother-in-law in the unfamiliar environs of Bethlehem, chose to accept whatever God provided and expressed gratitude for the simplest kindness of Boaz. She never forgot that she was a foreigner, undeserving of the least favor from anyone.

Like little Richie in the *Dick Van Dyke Show*, who squealed with glee when his dad returned home from work and reached into his pocket, producing the only present he had brought home for him that day—a paper clip—it shouldn't take much to make us grateful.

As Matthew Henry said so beautifully, "When we have no other answer to the suggestions of grief and fear, we may have recourse to this: 'I thank Thee, O Father.'"[6]

What a difference gratitude makes.

> **MAKING IT PERSONAL:** *As a rule, are you easily contented with what God provides, or do you find yourself resenting difficult circumstances or people and becoming demanding or depressed when others fail to meet your expectations?*

A SURE CURE FOR COMPLAINING

A grateful heart will be revealed and expressed by thankful words, while an unthankful heart will manifest itself in murmuring and complaining.

True story. A church group from New Bern, North Carolina, had traveled to the Caribbean on a mission trip. As you probably know, the conditions at the posh, luxury resorts are a far cry from the impoverished way of life endured by many others on these tropical islands.

During this particular ministry trip, their host took them to visit a leper colony on the island of Tobago. And while there, they held a worship service in the campus chapel. As you can imagine, the sight of emaciated lepers filing into their seats on the bare pews bore deeply into the minds and memories of each visitor to this unaccustomed scene.

But no memory left its mark like this one:

When the pastor announced, "We have time for one more hymn. Does anyone have a favorite?" he noticed a lone patient seated awkwardly on the back row, facing away from the front. At this final call for hymn requests, with great effort, the woman slowly turned her body in the pastor's direction.

"Body" would perhaps be a generous description of what remained of hers. No nose. No lips. Just bare teeth, askew within a chalky skull. She raised her bony nub of an arm (no hand) to see if she might be called on to appeal for her favorite song to be sung. Her teeth moved to the croaky rhythm of her voice as she said, "Could we sing 'Count Your Many Blessings'?"

> *Leave it to a grotesquely deformed leper to remind us that grateful people are characterized by grateful words.*

The pastor stumbled out of the pulpit, out the door, and into the adjoining yard, tears of holy conviction raining down his face. One of the traveling party rushed to fill his place, beginning to sing the familiar song in this unfamiliar place, arguably the most "unblessed" of any spot in the universe.

A friend hustled outside, put his arm around the sobbing pastor, and consolingly said, "I'll bet you'll never be able to sing that song again, will you?"

"Yeah, I'll sing it," the pastor answered, "but never the same way, ever again."[7]

Leave it to a grotesquely deformed leper to remind us that grateful people are characterized by grateful words, while ungrateful people are given to griping, complaining, murmuring, whining.

Some grumble at why God put thorns on roses, while others wisely notice—with awe and gratitude—that God has put roses among thorns. Hear what people are saying when they talk about the everyday events of their lives, and you'll see in an instant the difference between gratitude and ingratitude.

MAKING IT PERSONAL: *Do you spend more time counting and recounting your blessings or your problems?*

I'LL TAKE SOME OF WHAT SHE'S HAVING

Thankful people are refreshing, life-giving springs, while unthankful people pull others down with them into the stagnant pools of their selfish, demanding, unhappy ways.

Many people think of the Puritans as grim, joyless Christians. They are mistaken. In his 1859 book on the life and times of Puritan preacher Matthew Henry, Charles Chapman noted that:

> [Matthew Henry] possessed the desirable disposition and power of looking on the bright side of everything. . . . [T]here was a loveliness in his spirit, and a gladness in his heart, which caused others to feel "how happy a thing it must be to be a Christian." Though not given to indulgence he enjoyed the blessings of Providence with thankfulness. . . .

> [T]his cheerfulness . . . pervaded his entire life. . . . One reason of the great power of his life over many who were not decidedly religious men, lay in the constancy of that happy spirit which they saw and coveted.[8]

I've acknowledged that my natural "bent" is to react to people and life's circumstances in a negative way. When I'm asked how I'm doing, the first thing that pops into my head is often a burden I'm carrying, a hurt I'm harboring, or a deadline I'm working under. As a result, I'm afraid people who hang around me for any length of time may find themselves thinking how difficult and wearisome it is to be a Christian and serve the Lord. Matthew Henry's testimony challenges me deeply and causes me to want what he had–to have the kind of disposition that causes others to feel "how happy a thing it must be to be a Christian!"

We all know what it's like to be around people who consistently view life through a negative lens. Those are the ones we avoid and steer clear of. We've got enough to worry about ourselves without being weighed down any further by someone else's litany of complaints, don't we?

Not that there aren't times when it's appropriate to share our troubles with a caring friend. Not that "Fine" should always be the default when we're asked how things are going. But before I begin to pour my problems into anyone else's lap, I want to share first how good God is and how blessed I am to be called one of His children.

To be grateful.

As I said before, it's a difference you can see. And feel.

Ingratitude is toxic. It poisons the atmosphere in our homes and workplaces. It contaminates hearts and relationships. Moms and dads can break the spirits of their children with it, and husbands and wives can deaden every sensitive emotion in the mate they once swore at a church altar to love and to cherish from that day forward. We can be obsessive about spritzing away the disease-carrying, odor-causing bacteria from our tables and countertops, but nothing is more contagious in our homes than an ungrateful spirit.

Well, maybe one thing is.

Gratitude, I'd say, is equally as contagious as its evil twin. If you're sick and tired of living in a home where all the joy and beauty has been sucked out through negative, unappreciative words and attitudes, you can make a change. You can become the kind of person you've always wanted to be around. The kind of person who makes the Jesus and His gospel winsome to all who come within the reach of your grateful, "happy spirit."

> **MAKING IT PERSONAL**: *What impact does your spirit have on those around you? Are they refreshed and encouraged by your thankful spirit? Or are they weighed down by your negative, ungrateful words and attitude?*

Two kinds of people: grateful and ungrateful. Worshipers and whiners.

But only one kind, like Fanny Crosby, can lift her blind eyes toward heaven and exclaim in song and spirit, "Perfect submission, perfect delight, visions of rapture now burst on my sight."

Which kind of person are you? Which kind of person do you really want to be?

* * *

If you've read this far, I'm believing that God has been at work in your heart, exposing any roots of ingratitude, and giving you a fresh desire to be a grateful person. At this point, you may be thinking, "I want to be more grateful . . . but how?" I'm so glad you asked!

CHAPTER SIX

How Can I Say
Thanks?

Gratitude is born in hearts that take time
to count up past mercies.

CHARLES JEFFERSON

It was sacrifice enough for Brad Morris to travel all the way from Texas to attend his friends' wedding in Las Vegas. (After all, they weren't old schoolmates of his, simply coworkers he'd gotten to know and like.) Add to that the generosity of sending them off with the open-ended gift of a crisp, new $100 bill. Sure, it wasn't a five-piece place setting or a stem of their chosen crystal, but for a bachelor trying to honor the happy couple with his best wishes on their future marriage–I don't think Miss Manners would harrumph too loudly at that.

So you can't help but sympathize with his sentiments when, about a month later, an email arrived in his inbox with the catch-all opening line: "Dear Friends." The senders of this cyber-message went on for a brief moment, thanking the whole lot of them for attending their recent wedding and, by the way, "thanks for all the nice gifts."

"Cheap and pitiful" is how Brad described his friends' ten-minute attempt at getting gratitude off their to-do list. "I would just as soon have received *no* thank-you as to receive *that*."

But this is all part of a downhill trend reported in an article in *USA Today*,[1] which pointed out that sincere and thoughtful thank-you notes are increasingly being replaced by (if anything at all) an email that amounts to a mere confirmation of receipt.

For some this may stem back to their childhood, when their parents sat them down after Christmas and birthdays and gave them a grid to work with: "Dear (blank). Thank you for the (blank). I love it! Signed, (blank)." Nobody honestly believed the thanks was all that genuine; it was just a matter of "good manners." When they became adults—old enough to decide for themselves whether they wanted to keep up this charade—many of them saw no purpose in continuing something that had so little meaning.

Given the general level of disinterest in old-fashioned note writing today, it's no wonder that some now feel that a pecked-out email is going above and beyond.

But gratitude is much more than checking a list or completing a transaction. We've read our Bibles enough to know that God is not pleased with technical, bare-bones attempts at obedience. We cannot expect true blessing for merely fulfilling a duty-bound sense of obligation. God's desire is not just to see us *doing grateful things* but to see us doing grateful things out of the overflow of *a truly grateful heart*.

If our thankfulness never becomes more than fulfilling the minimal obligation, if we never outgrow the rote mindlessness of fill-in-the-blank thanks, we stop short of experiencing that grace

-filled lifestyle of genuine, heartfelt gratitude.

It's time to get to the heart of gratitude, to let it become more than the perfunctory note writing we may have learned as kids. Are you tired of being a whiner? Are you ready to be a worshiper? Are you convinced that ingratitude is not only a bad habit, but a grievous sin against a good God and a poor reflection on His gospel and grace? Are you ready to become the kind of person who brightens your home, church, or workplace with the fresh air of gratitude rather than constant complaints and criticism?

In this chapter we'll explore some practical ways to cultivate that heart. Not just formally and officially, but as a newfound lifestyle.

SPEAK UP

Perhaps you've heard about the Vermont farmer who was sitting on the porch with his wife of forty-eight years, just beginning to realize what a great partner and help she had been to him all these years and how much she meant to him. He turned to her and said, "Wife, you've been such a wonderful woman that there are times I can hardly keep from telling you!"[2]

There are probably many moments throughout the day when a grateful thought pops into your head. Perhaps you find a $20 bill you didn't know about that had fallen to the bottom of your purse. Perhaps the person you called to help solve a problem with your cell phone bill was actually courteous, helpful, and graciously handled your complaint. Perhaps the rain that was forecast (which would have spoiled your plans for the afternoon) went north of town instead and left you with a delightfully sunny day for carrying out your plans.

Occasions for gratitude are all around us. If we recognize them at all, our general reaction is to let the thought we hear in our minds suffice for our gratitude. But the Bible says, "Let us continually offer up a sacrifice of praise to God, that is, *the fruit of lips* that acknowledge his name" (Hebrews 13:15).

My responsibilities sometimes require me to drive over a bridge that spans the Arkansas River, first thing in the morning. Numerous times, I have been enthralled by the sight of the sun coming up over the river, sparkling on the rippling water, and have not been able to restrain myself from saying aloud, "*Thank You, Lord,* for this scene—it's beautiful!"

Similar words of thanks often rise from my heart to my lips in other settings—after listening to a sermon that has spoken to my heart in a powerful way, when touched by the kindness or generosity of a friend, when I receive some unexpected blessing or witness God's amazing grace at work in the life of another.

> If your pastor's messages encourage your heart and deepen your walk with God, don't assume he just automatically knows this.

Gratitude is not the quiet game. It begs to be expressed, both to God and to others. "Silent gratitude," Gladys Berthe Stern said, "isn't much use to anyone."

If a cashier has been unusually pleasant to deal with at the grocery store checkout, stop by to tell the manager what a delight you've found his employee to be, and how thankful you are for her attitude. He'll be glad to pass along the compliment, and she'll go home encouraged and freshly motivated about her work.

If a neighbor's flowerbed catches your eye every time you pull into the driveway, walk over and tell her how thankful you are for the hard work she puts into tending her yard and how it just seems to get more beautiful year after year.

If your pastor's messages encourage your heart and deepen your walk with God, don't assume he just automatically knows this or gets tired of hearing how his ministry is impacting people's lives. Look him in the eye and thank him for his faithfulness to bring you the Word, or jot him a note with a few specifics of how something he said really ministered to you.

> Does it really matter *if we actually verbalize* our thanks, as long as *it's in our heart?*

And, of course, when you're captivated by a glorious sunset, or comforted in sorrow, or uplifted by some sweet reminder of the hope God gives in the midst of life's many problems and challenges, make your praise ring not only in your head but on your tongue.

Yes, speak it out loud!

Why is that so important? Does it really matter if we actually verbalize our thanks, as long as it's in our heart?

I believe it does matter and that thankful thoughts need to be translated into thankful words. My mind goes to many psalms that exhort us to *speak* words of praise to God in the presence of others. Take a look at the highlighted words in these selected verses from Psalm 145:

One generation shall commend your works *to another*,
and shall *declare* your mighty acts. . . .

They shall *speak* of the might of your awesome deeds,
and I will *declare* your greatness.
They shall *pour forth* the fame of your abundant goodness
and shall sing *aloud* of your righteousness. . . .

All your works shall give thanks to you, O Lord,
and all your saints shall bless you!
They shall *speak* of the glory of your kingdom
and *tell* of your power . . . .

My mouth will *speak* the praise of the Lord,
and let all flesh bless his holy name forever and ever.

Convinced? Spoken words of praise and thanks have power to
dissipate that spirit of heaviness that sometimes weighs us down
and clings to us like a wet blanket. And they have power to do the
same for others. Further, I believe that spoken (and sung) worship
and thanks-giving can be instrumental in overcoming the lies and
schemes of the Enemy. In my own life, doubt, fear, confusion, and
anxiety have often been displaced and my spirit supernaturally lifted
and strengthened as I have spoken words of gratitude and praise.

SING OUT

Another frequent theme of thanksgiving found in Scripture is its
musical side.

Psalm 28:7 says, "The Lord is my strength and my shield; in him
my heart trusts, and I am helped; my heart exults, and *with my song* I
give thanks to him." Psalm 147:7 picks up the idea: "*Sing to the Lord*
with thanksgiving; make melody to our God on the lyre!"

Gratitude is a tune you can dance to.

It certainly was for the Old Testament nation of Israel. I think
about that festive occasion when the walls of the city had been
rebuilt under Nehemiah's brave leadership, after all the hostility
and opposition they had endured to complete their work. "And at
the dedication of the wall of Jerusalem, they sought the Levites in all

their places, to bring them to Jerusalem to celebrate the dedication with gladness, *with thanksgivings and with singing*, with cymbals, harps, and lyres" (Nehemiah 12:27). Music and thanksgiving go hand in hand in the Bible.

You may be thinking, "Oh, I'm not much of a singer." Neither am I. (An audio technician's worst nightmare is when my speaking mic is on and I break out into singing in the middle of leading a conference session or giving a message!) But regardless of our natural musical talent or lack thereof, music is a powerful vehicle of our gratitude, a lifter of our heads. It doesn't have to *sound* good to *be* good.

Church service. Car ride.

Mowing the grass. Sweeping the patio.

The walk to the mailbox or to get the paper.

Anytime is a good time to sing your gratitude.

I was a piano performance major in college, although life has since limited the time I get to spend at the keyboard, and I don't often get to play anymore. But occasionally when I'm at home, I'll slip to the piano bench, open a hymnal, and begin playing through my favorites, one after the other, singing songs of praise to the Lord. My heart is refreshed just by singing to Him. (I've listed some of my favorite hymns on pages 225-26.)

At other times I may be reading a passage of Scripture, perhaps one of the Psalms, and I'll start singing the words, making up my own melody as I repeat these same words of thanks and worship back to the Lord. There's something about singing our thanks, not just talking it, that imbeds gratitude even more deeply into our souls.

So if you feel yourself slowly losing your appreciation for God and His goodness, try saying it with music.

KNEEL DOWN

"Dad Johnson" was a dear friend of mine, now at home with the Lord. Though a successful businessman, life had not always been easy for him. His mother died before he turned two. When he was in his mid-twenties, he lost his father. But Dad Johnson was the kind of person who, when I called him on his eighty-ninth birthday, said to me, "When I'm gone, if I'm remembered for anything, I want it to be that I was a grateful man." Was he ever!

Yet that grateful lifestyle was forged in the fires of affliction. And that fire was never more intense than when he and his wife faced the loss of their daughter Karen at the age of seventeen, less than two weeks before her high school graduation, in a fatal car accident.

Years later, when I was a seventeen-year-old college student, living in Ed and Joyce Johnson's home in southern California, I remember hearing Dad J recount a scene that occurred in the initial moments after he learned about Karen's death. None but those who have experienced such a sudden loss can truly begin to understand the depths of grief that must swell over you, the blur of thoughts, regrets, and reactions that press hard on every artery. I can't imagine.

But it doesn't take firsthand experience of tragedy to hear what happened next and be moved by the resilient power of a faith grounded in God's sovereignty and goodness. The Johnson family was spending the weekend at a vacation cottage in the southern California desert. Mr. Johnson saw a friend, accompanied by two other men, approaching the cottage and went outside to find out what they wanted. They broke the news to him that Karen's car had been hit by a drunk driver and she had not survived the accident.

The men went with Mr. Johnson into the house where he gathered his wife and four younger children together in the living room. He began by saying, "Before we ask God why He took Karen home in a head-on collision a few hours ago, *let's thank Him* for the seventeen years we had her." Astonishing. But true.

There's nothing wrong with being totally honest with God, coming before Him with our hurts and pains and intercessions, imploring Him to help and heal.

But prayer is more than asking. It is a vehicle of worship and gratitude.

Think about the overall makeup of your prayers. Are they out of balance in favor of asking and seeking? Are they top-heavy with complaints about your current condition or circumstances? Or–even in those times when you feel a desperate need for God's action and intervention–do your prayers include expressions of gratitude?

These are important questions to ask of ourselves, not to discourage honesty or deny reality, but to help train our hearts to see all that concerns us within the context of God's goodness and blessing. We must not forget His benefits while dealing with our problems. Even before His answer is in sight, thank Him–for being there, for listening, for working all things according to His will.

Paul said to Timothy, "First of all, then, I urge you that supplications, prayers, intercessions, *and thanksgivings* be made for all people" (1 Timothy 2:1). As surely as our "supplications" and "intercessions" are specific, heartfelt, and time-consuming, so should our "thanksgivings" be.

If you've always wanted prayer to be as natural as breathing, then pave the way with gratitude, and see if prayer "without ceasing" doesn't become your experience instead of your exception.

PRIVATELY AND PUBLICLY

For gratitude to become a true joy-maker in our hearts, it must be expressed everywhere, at every opportunity, both privately before

God and publicly before others.

The prophet Daniel is a great biblical example of someone whose gratitude occupied both his private and his public life.

After praying for God to show him the interpretation to Nebuchadnezzar's dream about the multimetaled statue with the feet of iron and clay, Daniel reacted to God's supernatural revelation–not by rushing out to tell the king as quickly as he could, thereby anchoring his position as the number-one wise man in the kingdom–but first by pausing to thank God for the answer.

> How grateful to *God are you when no one else is looking?*

"To you, O God of my fathers, *I give thanks and praise*, for you have given me wisdom and might, and have now made known to me what we asked of you, for you have made known to us the king's matter" (Daniel 2:23).

Once again, in the well-known affair of Darius's decree that all petitions for favor were to be directed toward the king alone for thirty days–the setup that eventually landed Daniel in the lions' den–his response to the threat revealed the characteristic pattern of his life: "When Daniel knew that the document had been signed, he went to his house where he had windows in his upper chamber open toward Jerusalem. He got down on his knees three times a day and prayed *and gave thanks* before his God, as he had done previously" (Daniel 6:10). Nothing could deter Daniel from his established practice of offering prayer and thanksgiving–even in the face of great danger.

How grateful to God are you when no one else is looking?

How quick are you to give thanks to God when everyone *is* looking? How much space does gratitude take up in your everyday interactions with others? Gratitude is not just for private consumption but for public conversation.

Have you ever been in one of those church services or small-group settings, for example, when the pastor or leader asks for testimonies of praise concerning God's goodness, and the room suddenly falls silent, as if everyone's too embarrassed to lead out or (perhaps) it's the first time the thought has crossed anyone's mind all week? We are often quick to share our concerns with others, but all too reticent to share our expressions of gratitude.

Yet David in the Old Testament was irrepressible when it came to public thanks-giving. "I will give thanks to you, O Lord, among the peoples; I will sing praise to you among the nations" (Psalm 57:9). "I will thank you in the great congregation; in the mighty throng I will praise you" (35:18).

Privately, to the Lord. Publicly, where others can hear and be reminded of God's goodness.

His grace is truly an all-season, all-weather, all-around wonder to behold. May our gratitude be no less remarkable.

WHEN AND WHERE

There are so many ways to express our thanks and praise. Through spoken words. Through music and song. Through prayers, in private, in public.

And there are just as many times and places in which to do it.

Holidays, for example. As you probably know, that word–"holiday"–comes from two words: "holy day." More than mere occasions for exchanging gifts or throwing parties, these are regularly scheduled, rhythmic opportunities to reflect upon and proclaim the goodness, the grace, and the keeping mercies of God. Christmas, Thanksgiving (naturally), and other points of celebration–from both the traditional and the church calendar–are ready-made milestones for marking time and making His praise glorious.

My most memorable New Year's Eves have been spent in a home with friends, celebrating God's goodness and giving thanks for His blessings of the year just completed, seeking His blessing on the year to come, and observing the Lord's Supper together (remember that "eucharist" means "giving of thanks").

The Old Testament Jews had their own holidays. Three times a year, every Jewish male embarked on pilgrimage to Jerusalem, primarily for the purpose of thanking the Lord. At the beginning of harvest, offering up the firstfruits of their annual yield, they would thank Him for what He had already provided . . . and for what He was sure to provide throughout the remainder of the year.

They would return again at Passover to commemorate and thank God for delivering their forefathers from slavery in Egypt. Then finally they would make a third trip at the end of harvest time, offering gratitude to God for the rains, sun, and seed that had transformed dry ground into provision and plenty.

There were other special days along the way for gratitude–the dedication of the temple, for instance, when the celebration and pageantry reached staggering heights of worship and thanksgiving.

Similarly, there are moments and markers in our own lives when gratitude is especially called for. In fact, those who know me will attest that it doesn't take much for me to find an "excuse" to call for a "thanks-giving celebration!"

Shortly after I moved into my first home, I invited friends and neighbors to join me for a special evening in which we all thanked God for His gracious provision in our lives and consecrated my home to be used for His kingdom purposes.

I remember another meaningful celebration that took place years ago. The invitation read:

> *You're invited to share in*
> *"A Celebration of Redemption"*
>
> *"Remember this day, in which ye came out from Egypt,*
> *out of the house of bondage;*
> *for by strength of hand the Lord brought you out from this place."*
> *(Exodus 13:3)*
>
> *On the occasion of my 35th spiritual birthday,*
> *I wanted to invite my friends to join in celebrating*
> *the great gift of salvation which is ours through Jesus Christ.*
> *This will be an informal time of praise, worship, and testimonies.*

The opening of a business. The beginning of a new ministry initiative at church. Birthdays and wedding anniversaries. Life is full of occasions that can be transformed from mere parties and pleasantries into deliberate moments of united gratitude. These are not just random events or passages of time. They are opportunities for giving thanks to the Giver of every good gift who "satisfies [our] years with good things" (Psalm 103:5 NASB).

Even funerals can be "holy days" that call for thanks for God's people. When my dad went home to be with the Lord on the weekend of my twenty-first birthday, we cried. We grieved. But we also gave thanks from full hearts—for the impact of his life, his love for us and the Lord, his sure home in heaven, and the promise of one day being reunited with him in the presence of Christ.

But it shouldn't take a special occasion for gratitude to spring up from deep within, as though it needs a grand stage on which to make its appearance. The Scripture calls us to all-day, everyday gratitude:

- *Morning and evening.* David instructed the Levites "to stand every morning, thanking and praising the Lord, and likewise at evening" (1 Chronicles 23:30).

- *Three times a day.* The example of Daniel, mentioned earlier in this chapter, was to come before God at morning, noon, and night, setting aside specific times of day to give thanks for His goodness and faithfulness.

- *The middle of the night.* "At midnight I rise to praise you," the psalmist wrote (Psalm 119:62). Moments of wakefulness through the night are calls to be mindful of the Lord, thanking Him again as we settle back to sleep on a soft bed of gratitude.

- *Continually.* "I will bless the Lord at all times; his praise shall continually be in my mouth" (Psalm 34:1). At every conscious thought of God's blessing, our automatic reflex should be–and really can be–instant gratitude.

And why not? After all, as David said, "I will give thanks to you forever" (Psalm 30:12). So why not start becoming proficient at expressing gratitude–not because we have to, not simply because we're commanded to, but as a reflection of truly grateful hearts.

* * *

So gratitude should be an every-moment, every-hour, every-day, lifetime event. Will we ever run out of things to be thankful for? Not a chance...

CHAPTER SEVEN

Thanks. . . for
Everything

*When thou hast thanked thy God
For every blessing sent,
What time will then remain
For murmurs or lament?*

R. C. TRENCH

You knew we'd get around to this eventually–the chapter on
"things to be thankful for." It's the one you may have expected to
meet you right up front, the one thing we usually ask around the
Thanksgiving table, the one you might spring on a children's Sunday
school class if the hour was running longer than you prepared for.

It's Gratitude 101.

"What are you thankful for?"

But there's a purpose in my leaving this off until the back half
of the book. It's the difference (again) between Christian gratitude
and its simple garden variety, between filling out the full address and
just stamping a blank envelope. Until we can make our thanksgiving

lists within the context of God's grace, it's like waking up in the night and only being able to see part of the clock. Knowing that it's "twenty after" really doesn't tell you much. But being able to match up hour and minute, like being able to match up gift and Giver, can keep us from "sleeping through" the whole gratitude experience.

I'm not trying to take all the fun out of this or to make it unnecessarily complex. I don't want to construct an elaborate methodology or machinery around this quite simple concept, as if only the wisest and most spiritual among us can really do it the way it's supposed to be done.

My desire is simply to free us to experience and express more of God's goodness, and to keep us from grieving His Spirit by failing to "recognize and express appreciation for the benefits we have received from Him and from others."

Who else but a Christian can thank someone for a good meal, a good time, or a good effort, knowing that this has not just been a gift to us from another person but ultimately comes from the living God?

I love knowing that He cares and provides for me, not just air to breathe and food to eat, but countless extras that simply flow from His generous heart.

And I don't want to miss thanking Him for a single one of them.

When my eyes are opened by gratitude to these boundless examples of grace, only then can I see clearly enough to press on in this broken world.

On the other hand, if we turn our gratitude for all these blessings away from the One who provides them, we're left with a handful of colorful thread—yes—but no pattern, no connection between them, nothing to arrange these scraps into anything truly useful or even just plain beautiful.

We're left with a bunch of "whats" but . . . "So what?"

VISIBLE, MATERIAL BLESSINGS

Therefore, as Charles Spurgeon said, "Let us daily praise God for *common mercies*–common as we frequently call them, and yet so priceless that when deprived of them we are ready to perish."[1]

Bath soap. Toothpaste.

Hot water. Dishwashing detergent.

Air conditioning. Houseplants.

Sunsets. Sunglasses.

Birthday cards. Blue skies.

Flashlights. Blankets.

Family photos. Fresh fruit.

Measuring cups. Warm clothes.

Books. Bookcases.

Beautiful music. Clean sheets.

Autumn leaves. Sticky notes.

If we take it all for granted, if we think life just shows up with this stuff already in place, if we trick ourselves into believing that everyday household items come from the grocery rather than from a gracious God, we walk right past countless reasons for worship without even knowing it.

People who draw a blank when asked what they're grateful for–after running through the fairly automatic litany of faith and family and food and health–can never be those who draw nearest to God, not when He has given us so many ways to answer this simple question.

Inkpens. Note paper.

Wildlife. Wildflowers.

Car insurance. Popcorn.

Attic space. Paved roads.

These aren't just nice to have. They're among the "every" good and perfect gift "coming down from the Father of lights" (James 1:17). They're included in the biblical appeal for "giving thanks always and for everything to God the Father in the name of our Lord Jesus Christ" (Ephesians 5:20).

People who remember to thank God for everything from pliers and pruners to paper plates are people who know what "everything" is all about.

And why shouldn't that person be you?

SPIRITUALLY SPEAKING

But even when ordinary gratitude is working hard not to leave one single blessing uncovered, all the way down to coat hangers and paper clips, there are places it simply cannot go, depths it cannot reach.

For if you think there are just too many things like this to keep track of and be thankful for, I ask you to start looking beyond the animal, vegetable, and mineral variety of God's gifts, and consider His spiritual blessings as well.

I assure you, this list is even longer.

One of the occasions I make a big deal about each year is my "spiritual birthday"—the day I first consciously trusted the Lord Jesus to save me. In 2002, when I celebrated my thirty-ninth spiritual birthday, I made a list of thirty-nine "spiritual birthday gifts"—gifts that according to His Word, He has given to me—and to all of us as His children. It was a great reminder of how much cause I have for gratitude. With the passing of years, I've continued to add to the list. And since His generosity is inexhaustible, I'm confident I won't live long enough to run out of gifts to thank Him for![2]

That list includes things like peace with God, being adopted into His family, being saved from His wrath, and having a purpose for living. I thank Him for giving me two great intercessors–both Jesus in heaven and the Holy Spirit within me. I thank Him for giving me an advocate, a defense attorney, who daily defends me against Satan's prosecution and accusations. I thank Him for restoring my soul, for giving me an inheritance with the saints, for His power to keep me from stumbling before the finish line. And the list goes on.

Only Christian gratitude, framed and contextualized within the matchless grace of God, can even hope to try wrapping its arms around so big a package. But let's try anyway, shall we? No telling what else we might find in this big pile of presents.

• *God's nearness.* "We give thanks to you, O God; we give thanks, for your name is near" (Psalm 75:1). Imagine if after reaching out to save us, God left us to work out this salvation of ours with "fear and trembling" all by ourselves. But, no, "it is God who works in you, both to will and to work for his good pleasure" (Philippians 2:13). It is His Spirit within us, nearer than our next breath, that both equips and encourages us to keep waging this battle of daily life. He's near when we call, near when we need Him, near when we stumble, near all the time.

I received an email from a woman who had attended a weekend retreat where they had erected a life-size model of the tabernacle for people to walk through. She wrote trying to describe how the experience of stepping into the symbolic Holy of Holies had impacted her. "I was overwhelmed," she said, "realizing so vividly again that I don't have to risk death when coming into God's presence like the Israelites did." The thick curtain of separation has been torn in two, top to bottom. Through what Christ did for us on the cross, we can now draw near to God.

God is near. Let us be grateful.

• *God's holiness and faithfulness.* Certainly there are times, prone to wander as we are, when God's relentless holiness feels more like a burden than a blessing. We find ourselves almost wishing that His flawless example and righteous requirements weren't always so rock-solid and unbending.

And yet what divine mercy, that even when our human natures might shortsightedly wish for some wiggle room inside His absolute standard of perfection, there is one thing in life we can always count on: God is holy and He is faithful. His holiness is more unshakable than the Rock of Gibraltar. While everyone else around us is subject to instability and change, He is always the same.

This steadfastness of God is not something to bristle at and quaver under. Rather, it is a gift, the "blessed assurance" that no matter how unreliable those around us may be, no matter how unstable our own footing, or how often or far we may fall, God will always be there, ever true, ever trustworthy. "Sing praises to the Lord, O you his saints, and give thanks to his holy name" (Psalm 30:4).

God is holy and faithful. Let us be grateful.

• *God's mercy.* Again, I am thankful that God doesn't lower His standards to accommodate our disobedience and inabilities. I'm glad that we can depend on Him to be the same yesterday, today, and forever. And yet, what a comfort it is to be reminded that "he knows our frame; he remembers that we are dust" (Psalm 103:14). Fully understanding–even better than we–that our best is nowhere near being good enough, "God, being rich in mercy" (Ephesians 2:4) has reached down to rescue and redeem us through the precious offering of His Son, the perfect sacrifice.

"I will give thanks to you, O Lord, for though you were angry with me, your anger turned away, that you might comfort me"

(Isaiah 12:1). With wrath being His justifiable response toward us, He has chosen to show mercy instead (see Habakkuk 3:2).

There is no way we could ever repay Him for such amazing grace. There is only one response that even begins to measure its worth—a thankful heart, expressed in both word and deed.

God is merciful. Let us be grateful.

• *God's salvation.* "But God shows his love for us in that while we were still sinners, Christ died for us" (Romans 5:8). "For our sake he made him to be sin who knew no sin, so that in him we might become the righteousness of God" (2 Corinthians 5:21). "Thanks be to God for his inexpressible gift!" (2 Corinthians 9:15).

When we consider the love of Christ, His incomparable sacrifice, and His gift of full redemption, sealed and secured forever, how can we let a single day pass without "giving thanks to the Father, who has qualified [us] to share in the inheritance of the saints in light" (Colossians 1:12)!

God has saved us . . . from sin and Satan and self. From darkness and destruction and death. Let us be grateful.

• *God's calling.* "I thank him," the apostle Paul said, "who has given me strength, Christ Jesus our Lord, because he judged me faithful, appointing me to his service" (1 Timothy 1:12).

Each of us has his or her own jobs to do. It may be managing a home and family, tending to patients, meeting the needs of clients and customers, teaching children, or one of a dozen different things. We also have the privilege of ministering to others on a personal level, preparing meals for families in crisis, visiting the sick and the elderly, sharing God's Word in a Bible study, and many other expressions of hands-on service. These are time-consuming. And they can be tiring.

In fact, I suppose if there's one common complaint I hear in my dealings with others–and in my own inner conversations with myself–it's the strain of busyness, weariness from the perpetual plate spinning.

But have you thought about being thankful for what I call "the blessing of meaningful work"? I realize some of that work may seem monotonous, menial, or meaningless. (For every exhilarating responsibility I enjoy, it seems there are ten or more that take sheer discipline to perform and for which there is no obvious or immediate reward.) Those tasks may leave you exhausted at the end of the day (or sooner!). For sure, every calling has its challenges that keep us humble and dependent on Him.

First Chronicles 1-9 is composed mostly of genealogies and lists–not one of those sections of Scripture we typically like to linger in! But recently I stopped to contemplate one paragraph that details the responsibilities of some of the Levites. Some were assigned to count the temple utensils every time they were used. Others "prepared the mixing of the spices" used for incense (1 Chronicles 9:30). And then there was Mattithiah, who was "entrusted with making the flat cakes" (v. 31). Not exactly job descriptions most would dream of having! But these faithful servants glorified God through embracing and fulfilling their calling, day in and day out.

As meaningless as some tasks may seem, as weary as we may get, we need to be reminded (*I* need to be reminded!) that it is a *privilege* to be entrusted by the living God with responsibility in His kingdom.

In the midst of relentless ministry deadlines and seemingly endless tasks, I find that the "burden" of my workload is lightened when I approach it as a high and holy calling, a gift to be received with gratitude.

Although He certainly doesn't need us to accomplish His purposes, God has called us into His service. Let us be grateful!

AND SO MANY OTHERS

- Victory over death and the grave. "Thanks be to God" (1 Corinthians 15:57).
- Deliverance from indwelling sin. "Thanks be to God through Jesus Christ our Lord!" (Romans 7:25).
- The ultimate triumph of the gospel. "We give thanks to you, Lord God Almighty" (Revelation 11:17).

Oh, there's really no end to this list.

His gifts to us are as boundless and endless as *He* is. In fact, I expect to spend the rest of eternity unwrapping those blessings! "Blessed be the God and Father of our Lord Jesus Christ, who has blessed us in Christ with *every spiritual blessing* in the heavenly places" (Ephesians 1:3).

RELATIONAL BLESSINGS

In addition to the spiritual blessings that come directly from His hand are those gifts that He sends by way of others–friends, family members, fellow believers.

In all but four of his New Testament epistles, Paul makes a point to give thanks for other people. Gratitude was a constant heartbeat of his ministry. He thanked them for their inspirational demonstration of faith, for their sacrificial expressions of love, for their example of unity and fellowship. Whenever he was personally encouraged by someone, he returned the favor with personal encouragement.

He considered these people and relationships to be priceless treasures.

I have many of these treasures myself. Family members. Faithful, diligent colaborers for Christ. Ministry partners. Dear friends who bless me with their acts of kindness, their prayers, and their encouragement to persevere in the battle.

Have you ever made a thorough inventory of the people who have touched your life? Have you taken time to thank them?

William Stidger was a middle-aged pastor, struggling like so many others through the heavy, leaden days of the Great Depression. Everywhere around him were the forlorn looks and downtrodden dispositions of men and women aching for the basics—a job, a decent meal, an ounce of security.

> Have you ever made a *thorough inventory of the* people who have touched *your life? Have you taken* time to thank them?

It couldn't have been easy pastoring in days like that (not that it's easy pastoring in any generation). But one day while sitting around a table with a group of friends who were bemoaning the dire straits people found themselves in— even provoking some to consider taking their own lives—William made up his mind that he would choose to be thankful. Thankful for God, for faith, and for the people in his life.

Oddly, the first person who crept into his thoughts was an English teacher, the one who had first inspired in him a love of literature and poetry, a passion that had certainly played a significant role in preparing him for his calling as a pastor and writer. He sat down that evening and composed a simple letter of thanks to her, dropping it off for posting the next morning.

Within only a few days' time, he received by return mail a feebly scrawled note from this very teacher. It started off, "My dear Willy,"—he hadn't been called by that name in years—"I can't tell you how much your note meant to me. I am in my eighties, living alone in a small room, cooking my own meals, lonely, like the last leaf of autumn lingering behind.

"You'll be interested to know," her letter continued, "that I taught in school for more than fifty years, and yours is the first note of appreciation I have ever received. It came on a blue, cold morning, and it cheered me as nothing has done in many years."

Needless to say, such eloquent sentiments brought a lightness into William Stidger's chest that hadn't been there the day before–the kind of carefree joy that had seemed almost nonexistent since the stock market crashed and took everything else with it. Or so it appeared.

Then, motivated and energized by this response to his expression of gratitude (thankfulness is invigorating to recipients and givers alike!), he thought of someone else, a kindly old bishop who was now retired and whose wife had passed away in recent months. He was a man who had often given William counsel and good guidance over the years, especially early in William's ministry. Perhaps now was a good time to say thanks.

Again, only a couple of days passed between one note and another, as William's thoughtful words inspired an immediate and grateful reply. The elderly bishop, writing in response, said, "Your letter was so beautiful, so real, that as I sat reading it in my study, tears fell from my eyes, tears of gratitude. Before I realized what I was doing, I rose from my chair and called my wife's name to share it with her, forgetting she was gone.

"You'll never know how much your letter has warmed my spirit. I have been walking around in the glow of your letter all day long."[3]

The glow generated by sincere gratitude.

Those whose hearts are tuned and alert will never lack reasons to say "Thank you!" Physical and material blessings. Spiritual blessings. People who have blessed and touched our lives.

"Blessed be the Lord, who daily loads us with benefits, the God

of our salvation! . . . Bless the Lord, O my soul, and forget not all His benefits" (Psalm 68:19 NKJV; 103:2 NASB).

So then, as the songwriter put it:

Count your blessings, name them one by one,
And it will surprise you what the Lord hath done.[4]

* * *

When we stop to think about it, we truly are blessed people. But that doesn't mean life is easy. Sometimes our problems seem to outnumber (or at least outweigh) our blessings. Are we supposed to be like the orphaned Pollyanna who was forever playing The Glad Game? Can we really be thankful at all times, even when our eyes are filled with tears?

CHAPTER EIGHT

But Not without

Sacrifice

To give thanks to Him for all things, is, indeed, a very difficult duty;
for it includes giving thanks for trials of all kinds;
for suffering and pain; for reproaches; for loneliness.
Yet those who have learned submission will not find it a hard duty.

PRISCILLA MAURICE[1]

In 1989, photojournalist Tony O'Brien, a U.S. citizen, took an assignment from *LIFE* magazine to cover the fall of Kabul, the capital of Afghanistan, after the Soviets pulled out. He found himself caught in the crosshairs of a brutal civil war, and was clapped into an Afghan prison by Soviet-backed security forces.

Only those who actually endure wartime captivity can understand its horrors. Tony O'Brien, in fact, might not have been able to maintain his sanity throughout his own ordeal if not for the encouragement of a man who was incarcerated with him, a Shiite Muslim named Nader Ali. In the midst of their living nightmare, this remarkable friendship became the one bright ray of hope each of them needed to survive.

In time, various diplomats and colleagues succeeded in securing O'Brien's release, allowing him to return safely to his New Mexico home. But three years later, he found himself on board a plane bound for Kabul, back to the place of his imprisonment, back to the site of his unjust capture—not at the steely end of an artillery rifle . . . but at the relentless compulsion of gratitude. He wrote:

> The last time I saw Nader Ali, he was behind bars, watching me walk to freedom. I never thought I would see him again, never thought I would go back to Afghanistan. But now I am on a plane, returning to the place I spent the most terrifying weeks of my life. *He is a man I need to thank. . . .*
>
> I have thanked everyone else—those who got me out of prison, those who called my mother every day. Yet I never thanked the person who gave me the strength to live. Afghanistan is free now, but I am not.[2] (italics added)

For days, O'Brien traipsed through a city of 1.5 million people, with no address to guide him and few street signs posted—even if he'd known the one he was looking for. He didn't even know if the man he was seeking was still alive. And yet through a connection made here, a remembrance made there, his diligence was rewarded when he eventually found his man—Nader Ali. Alive. Surprised. Tony had risked it all, traveling halfway around the world to speak two simple words he just couldn't let go unsaid: "Thank you."

You're not likely to find thankfulness paired with such stories of sacrifice in your average candy and greeting card aisle (where gratitude is thought to live). But out in the byways of real life, a grateful heart must often strap on sword and shield, summon up its deepest courage, and brace itself for battle.

We've talked about gratitude from many angles in this book—what it is, what it isn't, what it means. But no discussion of Christian gratitude can be complete without being up-front and honest about something further—what it costs. And how it can survive—and thrive—in the midst of intense pain, loss, and adversity.

The late Romanian pastor Richard Wurmbrand, founder of Voice of the Martyrs, spent fourteen years in prison for preaching the gospel. Although his captors smashed four of his vertebrae and either cut or burned eighteen holes in his body, they could not defeat his will and spirit. "Alone in my cell," he testified, "cold, hungry, and in rags, I danced for joy every night."[3]

Charles Spurgeon—nineteenth century British pastor, writer, and seminary president, among a dizzying list of other responsibilities—suffered chronically with gout and rheumatism, suffered publicly from slander and ridicule, and suffered mightily with a dark level of depression that seemed to roar back at the worst possible times. Yet he grew to be thankful for these obstacles rather than allowing them to dominate or distract him. He once said in a sermon:

> I think that health is the greatest blessing that God ever sends us, *except sickness*, which is far better. I would give anything to be perfectly healthy; but if I had to go over my time again, I could not get on without those sick beds and those bitter pains, and those weary, sleepless nights. Oh, the blessedness that comes to us through smarting, if we are ministers and helpers of others"[4] (italics added).

Scottish preacher George Matheson (1842–1906) began losing his eyesight in late adolescence for no apparent reason. By age twenty he was totally blind, as a result of which his fiancée broke off their engagement. He struggled for many long months with a broken heart, wrestling with unanswered questions. The whole experience drove him nearly to despair and he was tempted to quit the ministry altogether. Yet ultimately he came to the place where he could say:

> My God, I have never thanked you for my thorn! I have thanked you a thousand times for my roses, but never once for my thorn. Teach me the glory of the cross I bear; teach me the value of my thorns. Show me that I have climbed to you by the path of pain. Show me that my tears have made my rainbow.

The Old Testament character, Job, suffered multiple, catastrophes in rapid succession as a result of marauders, lightning, and windstorms—his flocks stolen, his property destroyed, worst of all his seven sons and three daughters killed in a common accident. Upon learning of the massive losses, Job shaved his head and tore his robes. It was as though he was trying to cut away the memory and erase the news, perhaps find it was all a cruel hoax. But for a man accustomed to pointing his heart toward God, he couldn't just fall down and hope to die. Instead, he fell on the ground and worshiped. "The Lord gave, and the Lord has taken away; blessed be the name of the Lord" (Job 1:21).

> The capacity to *respond to adversity* with faith and gratitude *is not limited to* spiritual "superheroes."

But the capacity to respond to adversity with faith and gratitude is not limited to spiritual "superheroes" and biblical characters. For every Joni Eareckson Tada or Corrie ten Boom, there are countless others whose names and stories few have ever heard, who endure the worst that life has to offer and still come up thankful. Not unscarred, not unmoved, not functioning out of reality like robots, but still spotting reasons for hope and promise. They seem to know that the only thing more debilitating than what they're going through would be going through it ungratefully.

I hear from many of these brave individuals in emails and letters.

They tell of family histories filled with abuse and neglect, whole childhoods of instability and custody battles, and yet looking back on all that it cost them, they are grateful for what God has done.

Years lost to rebellion, deception, and apathy, still paying for their bad choices with frayed relationships and mountains of regret, yet able to rebuild on the backs of forgiveness and genuine repentance, and despite many things left to undo and repair, they are grateful for what God is accomplishing.

A wife whose husband quit loving her along the way and has left her alone with her shattered security and the stigma of single motherhood, yet she is grateful for the strength God provides for each day and the blessing of finding true love in Him.

I think of my dear friends Charles and Joann Archer, who have long served so well and faithfully in our ministry. In the summer of 2006, their lives were rocked with the staggering news that Joann had been afflicted with ALS. All too quickly, Joann's strength and capabilities ebbed away from her—her ability to speak, to feed herself, to lift herself into or out of bed. The week I completed this book, the Lord finally delivered her from the prison her body had become and took her home to heaven. Throughout the difficult ordeal, Charles regularly sent out emails, updating friends and coworkers on Joann's condition, and sharing specific prayer requests. In spite of so few positive things to report in those updates, I was struck by the way they were often signed at the bottom: *"Thankfully, Charles."*

No, the days don't always get easier. The nights can still drag until utter exhaustion finally pulls a person under for a few hours' sleep. But those who say "No" to resentment and "Yes" to gratitude, even in the face of excruciating pain, incomprehensible loss, and ongoing adversity, are the ones who really survive. They stand against the tide of memories, threats, loss, and sadness, and answer back.

With gratitude.

A Midwestern attorney who traveled to Houston to see his mother during the immediate days following Hurricane Katrina made time while he was there to go down to the hard-hit areas and see what he could do to help. His friends and work associates, aware that he was going, had pooled together several thousand dollars for him to turn into gift cards to hand out to any stranded victims he encountered.

Like everybody else who waded into the wreckage of Katrina's aftermath, he expected to find people grasping and angry, frustrations boiling over into street fights and raw survivalism. Instead, walking into the Astrodome where thousands were huddled to await their next move, he found a sense of calm and helpfulness and an orderly flow of charity and compassion. And even among those completely stripped of home and possessions, he discovered a startling measure of gratitude.

Meeting one family who had slept for several nights on the hard chairs and concourses at this stadium-turned-sanctuary, he sympathetically commented, "That must have been terrible." But the wife and mother of the group said, "No, not really." They had too much to be thankful for to complain. They had a roof over their head, enough food to eat, working lights, and each other. Not every family had been so fortunate.

Others told him stories of courageous sacrifice, of rescues that seemed almost humanly impossible, how all had seemed hopeless until someone had arrived to carry them out through waist- and chest-deep floodwaters. They didn't know what was next, but they knew to be grateful. Just to be there.

One older gentleman who had rescued twenty members of his extended family by floating them out on air mattresses, and who now kept all their combined belongings in a plastic bag under his makeshift cot, refused to take more than two of the man's gift cards for his five children and their families, not wanting to keep others from getting what *they* needed as well.

That's tough-going gratitude for you. In life's hardest, most unsettling times, many of these who had lost absolutely everything had found a surprising level of solace in the God-given perspective of gratitude.

We heard this same sentiment expressed in the aftermath of wildfires that swept through Southern California during the summer of 2007. Hundreds of thousands of acres were burned up, a half million people were evacuated, and more than two thousand homes were destroyed in the flames. Yet many of those who lived to tell their story found words of gratitude to describe their experience.

Sticking out of the ground in front of one of the ash heaps which used to be a family's home, a handwritten sign declared "Finally! No termites!"

And at a church service in Rancho Bernardo, where sixty families who had lost their homes gathered to give comfort to one another and to worship, one reporter noted, "They gave thanks for the big things: for lives saved, families, friendships. They also gave thanks for small things: a hug, a shoulder to cry on."

One of the fire victims was only able to salvage three boxes of photographs and her grandfather's cuckoo clock before fleeing the fiery onslaught. But on the Saturday before the Sunday service, as she searched through her home's ashes, she discovered a sundial her husband had given her. The following message was engraved on the sundial: "Grow old along with me. The best is yet to be."

"That says it all, doesn't it?" she mused. "We have a lot to be thankful for."

No matter what it costs.

THANKSGIVING WARS

Martin Rinkart was a seventeenth-century Lutheran pastor, serving in his German hometown of Eilenberg during the height of the Thirty Years' War. Being a walled city, Eilenberg soon found itself overrun with refugees and injured troops, inviting not only fear and overcrowding, but a deadly wave of disease and pestilence. Armies continued to march around its tight borders, besieging them of food and provisions, leaving the people in hunger and want.

The Rinkart home became a refuge of sorts for many of the sick and stranded. Though there was hardly enough for Martin to feed his own family, he ministered tirelessly to the endless needs of others around him, trying to match gaping need with God's care and compassion.

When other pastors fled for safety, Martin stayed on, eventually conducting more than 4,500 funeral services that year, sometimes over as many as forty to fifty bodies at a time.

One of them was his wife.

And yet at some point in the midst of such dire, disheartening

circumstances, Martin composed a family grace to be said by his
children before meals–a hymn that is still sung today all across
Germany at state occasions and national days of remembrance:

> Now thank we all our God,
> With hearts and hands and voices,
> Who wondrous things hath done,
> In whom his world rejoices;
> Who from our mother's arms
> Hath blessed us on our way
> With countless gifts of love,
> And still is ours today.

When we sing these words in the comfortable surroundings
of a Thanksgiving service at church, they seem picturesque and
idyllic. We smell turkey in the oven, warm bread on the table. We
hear the voices of relatives we haven't seen in months, perhaps since
last year, gathering around the house in pockets of reunion and
conversation.

But make no mistake: this joy-filled refrain wasn't birthed
around Thanksgiving feasts or in the settled quiet of a country cottage. Rather, it was forged in pain and suffering and grief and death.
It was a sacrifice of thanksgiving.

So it was for Dr. Helen Roseveare, medical missionary to the
Congo during the 1950s and 1960s, who battled fear, discouragement, and feelings of unworthiness for years, amid the high tensions
of this Central African region, where rebel armies posed a constant
threat to her team's work and safety.

In August of 1964, the worries became reality; word spread that
the local chief had been abducted and flayed alive–not only killed

but eaten.[5] Then came the night when Helen and the other women missionaries who had not already fled the country were seized at gunpoint by guerrilla soldiers who took over the hospital compound and occupied it for five months. The women were savagely beaten, humiliated, and raped by the rebel soldiers.

She has never forgotten that first very dark night: "I felt unutterably alone. For a brief moment, I felt God had failed me. He could have stepped in and prevented this rising crescendo of wickedness and cruelty. He could have saved me out of their hands. Why didn't He speak? Why didn't He intervene?"[6]

> The question that came to her heart was: "Can you thank Me for trusting you with this experience, even if I never tell you why?"
>
> —HELEN ROSEVEARE

But in the midst of that terrifying ordeal, as she cried out to the Lord, she sensed Him saying to her, *"Helen, can you thank Me?"* She knew God was not asking her to thank Him for the *evil*, but the question that came to her heart was: *"Can you thank Me for trusting you with this experience, even if I never tell you why?"*[7]

Thanks-giving indeed comes at a cost.

The cost comes in different shapes and sizes and may be greater or less in different seasons of life. But we live in a fallen, broken world, and every season has its share of trials, ranging, as Elisabeth Elliot has said, from "traffic jams to tumors to tombs."[8] You're likely facing one or more of those trials right now. It may not be on the same order as what Martin Rinkart or Helen Roseveare endured. Nonetheless, for you to give thanks in your situation is not easy and would require a sacrifice.

You've been passed over for a position you felt you were the most qualified for. It was a job you really wanted, and it meant a pay raise you really needed. But now you've got to get up in the morning and go back to that same old job and turn the same old crank, around people who know you applied for something better and didn't get it ... and be grateful?

You slipped and fell getting out of your car on an icy morning, tearing cartilage in your ankle and landing you on crutches for up to three weeks. This is the last thing you needed with all the responsibilities you're carrying right now. It was going to be all you could do to keep up as it was. Now you may have to beg off some things you really wanted to do, and disappoint people you'd made commitments to ... and be grateful?

It's been one of those seasons when everything's been breaking all at once. The timing belt on the car. A water spot that showed up on the ceiling and, after a couple of estimates, is sure to mean a new roof and thousands of dollars. To add to your frustration, you'd just gotten some extra money in, hoping to pocket it away in savings and put the rest toward a vacation trip. Now you're paying it out in car and home repairs ... and you're supposed to be grateful?

I recall a season in my own life when I was deeply disappointed by a significant personal loss. For about eighteen months, I gave in to resentment and self-pity. A shroud of doubt and confusion wrapped itself around my mind and emotions, becoming progressively tighter and heavier, until I hardly knew what (or if) I believed about truths I had long held and cherished.

I knew in my heart that if I would only embrace His sovereign choice and cry out to Him for grace, He would be faithful to restore and reorient me. Instead I chose to nurse my wounds and held on to my "right" to wallow in the pain.

Looking back, I'm convinced that because I was unwilling to offer up "the sacrifice of thanksgiving" (Psalm 116:17), I sacrificed instead some of the sweetest, most precious moments I could have had with the Lord, allowing Him to prove Himself strong enough to meet my need with His tender love and compassion.

But I can tell you when and where the healing process started. It was on a hardwood floor in a mountain cabin in North Carolina, kneeling next to a wooden rocking chair, where I wept and finally cried out, "Lord, I still don't understand why You allowed these circumstances to come into my life. I don't know if I will ever understand. But I know that You are good, and whatever You do is for my good and Your glory. So by faith I choose to give you thanks."

> *My circumstances didn't change. But He changed me in the midst of them.*

The sense of sadness and loss did not immediately vanish. But as I surrendered my wounds and my will to Him, choosing to trust and thank Him, I began to experience release from the oppressive heaviness I had experienced for so many months. He began to restore, renew, and rebuild my spirit. And He started a process of transforming my loss into something of great spiritual value. Over time.

And today I can reflect on that period and those particular circumstances and see so much that God has done in my life as a result. Again, over time. The very loss I resisted and resented so intently, God has used to bring about rich blessing into my life.

That healing and release began when I said, "Lord, I'm willing to thank You for trusting me with this experience, even if You never tell me why." No, my circumstances didn't change. But He changed me in the midst of them.

I will ever be grateful for that.

THANKFUL THROUGH AND THROUGH

Are you facing a circumstance that just doesn't naturally call for gratitude? You're trying to be brave. You want to do the right thing. You've sensed the joy and vibrancy draining from your spirit. But trying to be thankful for what God is doing in your life right now . . . It's tough. *Really* tough. In fact, it seems impossible. In our own strength, *it is* impossible!

Thinking about this takes me back many years to my brother David's bedside in a Philadelphia hospital. There he lay–this younger brother who had always been so full of life and passion, the kid who was everyone's friend, from the school janitor to the school president.

He was the sixth of seven children in our home–I being the oldest. But because the seventh didn't arrive until a good while after his birth, he was for many years the baby in our family. Ah, David. The consummate "baby" of the family. Needing frequent reminders to turn in homework, to get to class on time (or at all), to go to bed at night. (He was usually tied up talking to someone who needed encouragement or help of some sort.) But always happy, it seemed, with hardly a care in the world and a heart as big as the world–a heart that beat passionately for God and for others.

David had just completed his junior year at Liberty University. He thought perhaps the Lord would one day have him be a missionary. He would have been a great missionary. He might never have buckled down to learn the language, but the people would have loved him, and he would have loved them to Jesus!

Called out of a meeting in Chicago that May day in 1986, I got the knee-buckling news that David had been in a serious car accident and wasn't expected to live. We should all come home immediately.

Later that day, we gathered in his room at the University of

Pennsylvania Hospital ICU. By this point, he had already been declared legally, medically, and clinically brain dead. Here was this athletic, robust young man, now ringed with wires and tubes and a breathing apparatus sustaining his heart for what we knew would be just a brief period of time.

The next seven days seemed like an eternity. If you've ever been there, you know.

We waited. We wept. We prayed. Then we received the news that his heart had finally stopped beating.

As we gathered around his hospital bed for the last time, one of our closest family friends opened his Bible and read from 2 Samuel, where King David was told that the son he had conceived with Bathsheba was dead. At first, his advisors feared telling him the news, thinking it would send him into a pit of despair. But gathering from their whispers and behavior that the worst had taken place, David did just the opposite of falling apart. He "arose from the earth and washed and anointed himself and changed his clothes. And he went into the house of the Lord and *worshiped*" (2 Samuel 12:20).

Our dear friend closed the Bible and said to us, "Our David is now dead. Now is the time for us to rise up and worship." And we did. Not because we felt like it, not because it was easy. We offered *a sacrifice of thanksgiving*. A sacrifice of faith. A sacrifice of which He is worthy.

Our hearts were breaking even as we tried expressing them. But what we were really saying was, "Lord, You've not given us the privilege of understanding why You would take this young life that was so devoted to You, and we may never understand Your reasoning this side of heaven. But Lord, we trust You. We know You don't make mistakes. And what we really want, even as we grieve the loss of son, brother, and friend–more than anything else–we want You to be glorified." And He has been.

The choice before you and me today is: Do we only give glory to God for the part of our life that's going the way we want? Or do we worship Him, trust Him, and give Him thanks, just because He is God—regardless of the dark, painful, incomprehensible places we encounter in our journey?

Look, it's a sacrifice either way. If we go on without gratitude—choosing to be bitter, constantly bemoaning our fate—we force ourselves to live in *already* unhappy conditions with the added drag of our gloomy disposition. Unwilling to stay mindful of the blessings we enjoy in spite of our difficulties, as well as the strength and sensitivity God grows best in us through hardship and loss, we sacrifice peace. We sacrifice contentment. We sacrifice relationships—and freedom and grace and joy.

> Anything that makes *me need God is* (ultimately, in the *truest sense) a blessing.*

But what if we could maintain all those things—and even increase them beyond anything we've ever experienced before—by making just *one* sacrifice: the sacrifice of thanksgiving?

I have learned along the way that, regardless of how I may feel, *anything that makes me need God is* (ultimately, in the truest sense) *a blessing.* Be it disappointment. Be it physical suffering. Be it mental or relational anguish.

And if you must go through what you're facing now anyway (should God choose not to lift it miraculously, which He can always do and we are always free to pray for), why make it even worse by withdrawing from His grace and fellowship, enduring life on the raw edge without relying on Him for help? Why not see what could happen if you let the pain drive you closer to His side?

Yes, to give thanks "in all things" may require a sacrifice. No, it may not change your situation, perhaps not even a little. But it will put you in the only possible position for experiencing everything God desires for you throughout this hard stretch of life.

And—beyond the tiny piece of horizon you can see from this momentary time and place—God's glory and grace will be seen even more brightly, as a result of your willingness to say with the psalmist: "I will bless the Lord at all times; his praise shall continually be in my mouth" (Psalm 34:1).

That's the promise of gratitude.

* * *

If you read this book from cover to cover, are moved by the stories, nod your agreement, even say, "That was a great book!"—and then simply move on with your life, my purpose in writing it will have failed. It is my intent to issue a call—and to answer that call myself—to a radically different way of thinking, living, viewing life, and responding to God's grace.

CHAPTER NINE

Going
Gratitudinal

*Gratitude consists in a watchful, minute attention to the
particulars of our state, and to the multitude of God's gifts,
taken one by one. . . . And all our whole life is thereby . . . filled with a
gladness, serenity, and peace which only thankful hearts can know.*

H. E. MANNING[1]

The way the story goes, a Hungarian man went to the local rabbi
and complained, "Life is unbearable. There are nine of us living in
one room. What can I do?"

The rabbi answered without hesitation, "Take your goat into the
room with you."

The man looked back at him as if he'd certainly misunderstood.
But he hadn't. "Do as I say," the rabbi insisted, "and come back in a
week."

Seven days later, the man returned, looking more distraught than
before. "We can't stand it!" he said to the rabbi. "That goat is filthy!"

"Then go home and let the goat out," the rabbi answered.

"Come back again in a week."

It was a radiant Hungarian who returned to the rabbi the following week. His whole demeanor spelled relief and refreshment. "How are you now?" the rabbi asked.

"Life is beautiful," the man answered. "We enjoy every minute now that there's no longer any goat–only the nine of us."

It's all in how you look at it.

It's a matter of attitude.

There's a buzzword used today to describe what takes place when a person adjusts the thought patterns that have become ingrained into his or her emotional makeup. It's called: "attitudinal change." It's a fancy way to say that new behaviors start with new mind-sets. The pathway to personal transformation requires a change in perspective.

I'd like to coin a new word for those who may be deficient in the gratitude department (which includes all of us from time to time).

I'm calling for "gratitudinal change."

That's because I want you to live in the fullness of your relationship with God, not hindered and hamstrung and holding Him at arm's length, but experiencing Him richly. Feeling at home in His presence.

I don't want you to be destroyed by the inevitable downturns of life–with no answer for the darts of unfair, unpleasant circumstances–a walking bull's-eye, just waiting for the next arrow to be shot in your direction. I want you to find the God-given reserve to stand strong in the midst of confusing, condemning onslaughts of opposition. I want your head up, lifted by the empowering Spirit of God within you, even when everything else within you is calling for a week in bed with the lights out and the blinds drawn.

I want your story to be rewritten into a tale of God's grace, one that He uses to help you be an effective minister of His hope and healing to those who are walking the same kind of path. I want you to be so available to His Spirit's leading, so aware of others' needs, and so willing to be open and genuine, that God takes the things Satan meant for evil and transforms them into things of value.

No one expects you to be superhuman. And certainly no one should ever make you feel as though gaining victory over your hardships requires acting like they don't exist, as if refusing to speak about them or make reference to them will cut off their blood supply. These losses or failures or injustices done against you are real. They are not dependent on your acknowledgment of them in order to breathe and attack. But just as certainly, they are no match for the greater plans and purposes of God. And when He is given room to work His will within you, He can be the One who puts the "supernatural" into your responses and reactions.

Yes, you.

That's why no matter who you are, where you've been, or what's happened to you along the way, you can be changed into a person who's known and marked by gratitude. God can do it in you.

Are you ready?

CHANGE IS GOOD

I started this book by recognizing that gratitude is often looked on as a lesser necessity in the Christian life. I disagree with that thinking entirely. But many of those who do value gratitude as an essential nutrient in growing one's Christian character may still consider it a mostly mental exercise. Primarily spiritual. More up-in-the-air than down-to-earth.

But I'm here to tell you that expressing true gratitude involves choices as practical as setting your clocks correctly, changing your vacuum bag, or locking your doors at night. It is a regular maintenance plan, something that only happens when you do it on purpose, yet it's sure to save you all kinds of trouble down the line.

It's hard work. But it works.

And we grow more like Christ every time we practice it.

So in an effort to help us grow "gratitudinally," I'd like to make several specific recommendations that can get us headed in that direction—and hopefully never turn back.

• *Surrender your rights to God.* Some years ago, I came across this challenging pledge by a late Bible teacher named Russell Kelfer. He suggested that it would be a good idea to write out this brief document on a piece of paper, sign your name at the bottom, and make a habit of recommitting yourself to it on a regular basis. It goes like this:

> Having been born into the kingdom of God, I do hereby acknowledge that God's purchase of my life included all the rights and control of that life for all eternity.
>
> I do further acknowledge that He has not guaranteed me to be free from pain or to have success or prosperity. He has not guaranteed me perfect health. He has not guaranteed me perfect parents. He has not guaranteed me perfect children. He has not guaranteed me the absence of pressures, trials, misunderstandings, or persecution.
>
> What He *has* promised me is eternal life. What He *has* promised me is abundant life. What He *has* promised me is love, joy, peace, patience, gentleness, meekness, and self-control. He has given me all of Himself in exchange for the rights to my life.

Therefore I acknowledge this day the relinquishment of all my rights and expectations, and humbly ask Him by His grace to replace these with a grateful spirit, for whatever in His wisdom He deems to allow for my life.[2]

Signed, you. Signed, me.

What a difference it would make if we started each morning not only worshiping the Lord and meeting Him in prayer and His Word, but establishing from the very beginning of the day that He has full rights to our lives.

He has earned it, dear one. The guilt-to-grace-to-gratitude model we talked about earlier is not only in keeping with a biblical theology and lifestyle, it is crucial to our joy. Surviving on God's undeserved mercy but rarely being floored at the majesty of this eternal transformation He has accomplished in us is incompatible with abundant life. If we are to bloom and flourish as children of God in this harsh and suffocating culture—shining like "lights in the world" (Philippians 2:15)—we must pour ourselves out as a drink offering before the Lord. Only then will we "take hold of that which is truly life" (1 Timothy 6:19).

It's not our stuff, it's His.

It's not our house, it's His.

It's not our place to make demands and call the shots. It's His. And when we learn to be grateful for that, we free ourselves to rest our full weight on the only sure thing this world has to offer.

Gratefully trust Him with everything. Make a gratitudinal change.

• *Commit to a set season of gratitude.* Unfortunately, reading a book on gratitude does not a grateful person make! And ungrateful people don't become grateful overnight. Nor do we become grateful by merely thinking about it or wishing to be more so. Like any other virtue, a grateful spirit is the work of God's Spirit within the life of a believer who is purposeful about putting off fleshly inclinations and cultivating spiritual ones. And that takes time, effort, and focused attention.

If you've read this far, I'm trusting that God has done a work in your heart and that you have a fresh, serious desire to develop a grateful heart. If that is the case, *please* don't do what we so often do when God speaks to us, and just move on to the next thing. If you do, you will allow the Enemy to steal the seed of the Word that has been sown in your heart through these pages (see Luke 8:12).

> Every blessing you *can think of, write it* down. See how long *the list might go.*

And don't make the mistake of thinking that a halfhearted, semiconscious effort to be more grateful is going to be fruitful. Any fruit that is borne is likely to be short-lived, if you don't do what it takes to develop a deeply established root system in this area of your life.

If you want to see lasting change—transformation—in this matter of gratitude, I want to encourage you to set aside a concentrated period of time to focus on that process. Determine the time frame, mark your calendar, and let your spouse or some other accountability partner know that you are going to make this a season focused on gratitude. (They may want to join with you in the journey.)

How can you get started? You may want to adjust your Bible reading during that time, using a concordance or a topical reference Bible to guide you to Scriptures on thankfulness that you could study and meditate on.

Or you could try journaling your blessings, both physical and spiritual. Everything you can think of, write it down. See how long the list might go.

One year for my birthday, a friend gave me a journal called *Counting My Blessings*, designed for this very purpose. The pages contained five blank lines for each day's remembrance. How long could it take to write down five things every day?

I kept that up for the better part of that year. It was a rich season of gratitude. And now, whenever my tank's running a little low, I can go back and read back over those daily lists of blessings. Page after page. Instance after instance. Tangible reasons for being grateful to God upon every remembrance of His goodness.

What a gift of worship and thanks to the Lord, not to mention a gift to yourself—even to your children and grandchildren and others who might one day read your lists themselves and be encouraged to choose gratitude.

In order to help you in this process of gratitudinal transformation, at the end of this book I've included a 30-day devotional guide. It's designed to give you a track to run on as you set aside a month to let gratitude be a centerpiece of each day, a priority in your thinking and interactions. If you'll take this 30-day "gratitude challenge," I'm confident you'll look back a month from now and find that you're looking at life through different lenses and that God has done a fresh work of grace and gratitude in your heart.

• *Take stock of your gratitude accounts.* Who deserves (or needs) a word of thanks from you? Who in your life could use a bit of encouragement today?

Your husband or wife? Your children? Your parents?

Your brothers and sisters? Aunts and uncles? Nieces and nephews?

Your pastor? A teacher? Coworker? Boss? Your best friend? Small group leader? Prayer partner?

What about the neighbor who takes your trash to the curb on days when you're out of town? What about the auto mechanic who keeps your car in good running order? What about the older woman in your hometown church who always made a point of speaking to you when you were growing up, and who still causes you to feel like it makes her day when you're back for a visit and she gets to see you?

Sure enough, their funeral will roll around one day and—if you're able to go—you'll sign the book and stand with the floral arrangements, swapping stories with the survivors and recalling what this person meant to you throughout your life. But how much sweeter would it be to feel their hand in yours, pat them gently on the back, and watch their eyes light up as you tell them face-to-face what their life has meant to you?

One of my favorite "gratitude account" stories involves a homeless man named George, who lived in a rented room at a Chicago YMCA and spent his mornings napping in an old metal chair in the back of a police precinct, where he had become something of a fixture.

Two of the officers had grown kind of fond of the old fellow, who wrapped his shoes in rubber bands to keep the soles from flapping, and draped himself in a threadbare overcoat that did little to ward off the Midwestern winter chill. The two policemen would sometimes slip him a few bucks to help him on his way, even though they knew that Billy the Greek, owner of the nearby G &W Grill, was in the daily habit of fixing George a nice, hot breakfast, free of charge. Every day.

When Christmas arrived one year, the two officers and their families decided to invite George over for dinner. And while he was there, they pulled out several presents for him to unwrap, just like the others in their family.

As they drove him back to the Y later that evening, George asked if they could swing by the G &W first. Sure enough, the light was on and Billy was inside. And as they let George out of the car, his arms full of boxes he had been quietly rewrapping in the back seat, they watched in disbelief as George walked up to this kind short-order cook at the greasy spoon, and said, "You've been good to me, Billy. Now I can be good to you. Merry Christmas," he said, placing every single present in the arms of his friend.[3]

So keep track of your balance. Double-check for any unrecorded entries. And set aside ample time to monitor the books. Make sure that everything's paid up.

For a change.

• *Write thank-you notes.* Though many no longer consider this a necessary practice, it's still true that caring enough to write a letter, buy a stamp, and look up an address, just to say thanks, is a kindness that reflects a heart of grace and humility. Further, the act of expressing gratitude breeds *joy.* In the sender and in the recipient.

You've probably been on both ends, as have I. How often God has ministered tailor-made, timely grace to my heart, in the form of a hand-addressed letter amid all the credit card applications and department store circulars in the mailbox. And how often has He released me from self-absorption and discouragement as I have paused to write a note to someone who has been a means of grace in my life.

It's a sure-fire double blessing.

I try to carry around some blank thank-you notes with me, just in case I find myself with a few stray minutes at some point in the day. That's really all it takes—just five or ten minutes—to remember someone who's blessed your life in some manner or fashion, then jot down your heartfelt sentiments, and send it on its way. So simple.

And yet so transformational. I saw this in real life when some dear friends of mine nearly lost their twenty-nine-year-old son Jeff in a car wreck. For two weeks afterward, once his survival seemed at least shakily secure, all signs pointed to serious, long-term impairment. His injuries simply were not the kind that people walk away from unscarred for life. But on the wings of fervent prayer by scores of their friends and family back home, God miraculously intervened with healing and rapid recovery, defying the odds and astonishing the medical staff who were tending to Jeff's critical needs.

On the long drive back from the St. Louis hospital to their home in Indiana, where his parents would be caring for him while he continued his recuperation, Jeff began to deal with how far he had drifted from his childhood faith and how close he had come to pushing the outer limits of rebellion. At one point, sitting in the backseat, he asked his mom and dad if they would tell him what really happened that night of the accident and in the days immediately following.

Through tears of traumatic remembrance, they shared how they had first heard the news, how they had rushed down to be with him, how they had rallied prayer support by phone as they hurtled along the highway. They told how his sister and two brothers had lain prostrate over his unconscious body for entire nights at a time, crying out to God to spare his life. They told of friends who had dropped everything and traveled great distances to be there by his bedside, offering every practical and spiritual service imaginable during this time of reeling emotion.

Suddenly the front-seat report was cut off as Jeff broke into uncontrollable sobbing. Overcome by what God had done, what his family had been through, what so many had sacrificed . . . it was too much to hold in any longer. Although he had done nothing to deserve this kind of concern, he had been the recipient of an outpouring of grace and love, freely given.

When finally able to settle his emotions, Jeff reached for his cell phone to call his siblings, to thank each of them for being there when he needed them most. Then, wrapping up his last call, he asked his dad to pull off at the next exit. Wheeling into a Walmart, he sent them in for thank-you notes. And the whole way home, he went through package after package, writing from his heart, spilling out his gratitude with pen and ink.

I remember his mom and dad telling me how earnestly he kept this up after they got home, eventually writing more than a hundred notes to those who had prayed for his recovery and–even more–for his spiritual restoration. Grace had come in like a refreshing spring, and gratitude just kept rushing out in equal torrents.

Thank-you notes are a tangible way to communicate what is (or should be) in our hearts. A way to express appreciation for the benefits we have received from others–gifts, acts of service, godly example and counsel, prayers, encouragement, etc.

Do those notes have to be handwritten? What about email (or, for my younger friends, Facebook, texting, Twitter, or whatever other electronic medium I haven't caught onto yet)? For many of us, electronic communication is the quickest and easiest way to send a message. I often send emails expressing gratitude to a friend or colleague. And I am always appreciative to be on the receiving end of those kinds of emails. Certainly there's no one "right way" to say "Thanks."

But in this high-tech era, I still believe nothing quite says it like a "real letter," whether typed or handwritten. (I generally send handwritten notes, although I confess that in my case, typed notes would more easily be deciphered by the recipients!)

Don't get hung up on the "technique." *Do* resolve to have a thankful heart and to take time to express your gratitude as frequently as possible, by whatever means possible, to as many people as possible. When I think of how often God has used notes of gratitude from others to encourage and strengthen my heart, it makes me wonder who else may have needed a word of encouragement that I failed to send in response to the prompting of God's Spirit.

I think the apostle Paul (a prolific thank-you note writer himself) would rejoice to see that we got what he was saying—that those who sow bountifully are also the ones who get to reap bountifully, "overflowing in many thanksgivings to God" along the way (2 Corinthians 9:6–15).

> One of the most *meaningful exercises* a family or group *can do is to commit* to a season of *thankfulness together.*

I challenge you, if you're not already in the habit, to pursue this goal with relish. Perhaps you could keep some cards by your bed, or your desk, or wherever you're most likely to put them to use. If you want to run one of gratitude's most enjoyable and encouraging errands, keep your stationery stash well-stocked. It's a can't-miss investment in others.

It's positively gratitudinal.

• *Do it together, as a Body-building exercise.* One of the most meaningful exercises you could do as a family, a Sunday school class, a Bible study group, a group of coworkers, or perhaps an entire church, is to commit to a season of thankfulness together.

Deliberate, targeted, Holy Spirit-directed expressions of gratitude.

Make it the emphasis of both your personal and corporate worship. Ask God to grow in you and your group a grateful spirit—more grateful for His grace, His guidance, and His salvation, as well as growing in gratitude for the little things we overlook.

One of the apostle Paul's main concerns, you recall, was his burden for the unity of the body of Christ. He knew that few things provided a more compelling example of what Christ could do in a person's life than the oneness of drastically different people, all beating to one kingdom pulse and rhythm. He knew that a church united in mission–not just in the leadership but throughout the entire body–could truly hear from and move to the heartbeat of God.

If your family, group, or church were to develop a corporate sense of gratitude, how many petty squabbles would disappear? How many people, who have been at odds with each other, would find a reason to put an end to their selfishness and strife? How many ministries would be revived into true usefulness, simply by being populated with grace-filled men and women growing ever more grateful for the privilege of serving Him–together?

That would be a welcome change, now, wouldn't it? I'd call it a gratitudinal change. And I'm calling for it today.

(Would you allow me to take a quick rabbit trail here? Every demographic within the body of Christ needs to be intentional about cultivating an attitude of gratitude. But I think this focus is particularly important for those of us who are older, unmarried women. As I've watched women age, I've seen how proactively pursuing gratitude can help counter an otherwise natural tendency to become negative, brittle, severe, isolated, bitter, whiny older women–women who make life unpleasant for themselves and others. I believe that a humble, grateful woman who walks in community with other believers will become increasingly gracious, warm, large-hearted, and yes, beautiful–inside and out. Just a note of caution and encouragement –to myself and anyone else who may fit the category!)

PLACES TO GO

In appealing for gratitudinal change, I am not calling you to something that's trivial and inconsequential, much less something that's contrived or insincere. When gratitude becomes your default setting, life changes. As we've said earlier, the whole world looks different when you see it through gratitude-colored glasses. A problem that used to bury you now takes its rightful place behind twenty other blessings that are bigger than it'll *ever* be. A recurring issue that once brought out a whole range of pent-up emotions now only produces a new excuse for praising God with greater fervor than ever, knowing He is more than true and trustworthy.

> When gratitude *becomes your default* setting, life changes.

Gratitude changes things.

But first, you need to tell God you're going there. Tell Him you're going to begin letting your salvation be more than a once-upon-a-time event, but rather a daily cause for celebration and wonder.

Tell Him you're going to make each day a fresh opportunity to watch for His blessings in things both great and small—from the ultimate, awesome gift of His saving grace, to the privilege of having a healthy family, to the pleasure of not having one of those little painful sores you can sometimes get in your mouth. (Has it occurred to you to be grateful for that recently?)

Tell Him you're going to offer up to Him every situation and circumstance in your life, even the ones that are still sensitive to the touch, the ones that make absolutely no sense, the ones you just really don't understand why you're having to put up with right now. No matter how bad it gets, no matter what someone says to you, no matter how long it goes on or where it might lead, you will drop the full weight of it at His feet every night, be thankful for His strength that brought you through the day, and wait for His mercies that will be new in the morning (even though you may start needing them again at 12:01)!

Arguably the most affluent, materially blessed people in the history of the world, we have become angry, bitter, proud, and ungrateful. We have gotten this false sense of entitlement and the entirely unbiblical idea that God owes us ease and luxury or at least the chance to go for two weeks without having to deal with this one particular matter that is so difficult or discouraging. We can hardly conceive of our spiritual forebears (and brothers and sisters around the world in our own lifetime) who have gone to their martyrdom singing hymns of praise to God.

Listen, dear friend, God loves you, His promises are sure, and your heavenly destiny is settled forever if you've trusted Christ Jesus as your Lord and Savior. But some of the holy work we need to have done in us and through us can only come through the valley of shadow and suffering. Are you going to be resistant to that? Or are you going to be clay in His hands, knowing that He is intent on shaping you into the image of Christ and wants to use your life for something far bigger than your own comfort, convenience, and pleasure? He wants your life to be part of a grand, eternal redemptive picture that portrays the wonder of His saving grace. One day that picture will be complete and together we will magnify Him forever.

In the meantime, we can go surrendered and willingly, trusting God and His higher ways, or we can go kicking and screaming. The choice is ours.

I want us all to go forward in ways that are pleasing to Him, ways that place us in the center of His great will and plan. So I say to you, and I say to myself: let's go humbly, in faith, and on bended knee.

And for our own good and His glory, let's go gracefully.

And gratefully.

A Personal PS:
For those who feel, "I just can't give thanks in all things!"

As you've read this book, you may have found yourself convicted about roots of ingratitude in your heart. Perhaps you've been challenged by the call to cultivate a lifestyle of "giving thanks in all things." But there's a battle going on in your heart. You've just not been able to actually take the plunge and wholeheartedly say "Yes" to that challenge.

It may be that there is a particular circumstance in your life that seems outside the reach of thankfulness. Or it may be that you know you need to be more grateful, but find yourself still wanting to stop short of "putting off" *all* complaining–of unreservedly committing yourself to give thanks in *all* things.

If you can relate to any of that struggle, this PS is for you.

MY WRESTLING MATCH

Invariably, as I develop a new book or message, my own heart is confronted with the truths I am challenging others to embrace, and I am often brought to new or deeper levels of repentance.

When I first set out to write a book on gratitude, I somehow assumed this would be an "easier" topic to grapple with personally than other subjects I have written on in the past–themes such as *brokenness*, *holiness*, and *surrender*. (After writing books on those "heavy" topics, I quipped, "I want to write a book on *peace* or *happiness*!") Was I ever wrong!

Increasingly, as I spent weeks immersed in this manuscript, the Spirit of God shone His light into my heart and exposed some issues I wasn't sure I wanted to deal with.

That put me in a difficult position, because I have a commitment not to "speak" further down the road than I am actually "walking."

During the final days of the editing process, the conviction of the Spirit and the battle in my heart grew more intense. Finally, late one Saturday night, I felt impressed to compose an email, opening my heart to several friends to whom I have made myself spiritually accountable. Personal as it is, I've been encouraged to share some excerpts from that email with you. Here's what I wrote:

> I'm reluctant to release this book, due to the fact that there is a significant gap between some of its content and where my life is. I know the things I have written about choosing gratitude are true. But I still very much struggle to appropriate some of those things and live them out–i.e., to "choose gratitude and joy" when it comes to dealing with the things that stress and stretch me. The fact is, I am still reserving the right to "whine" rather than "worship" about things in my life that are hard.

I see some of my exhortations in this manuscript and think, "I know I'm not there–and I'm not sure I want to make those choices" (or more honestly and dangerously: "I don't want to make those choices, and don't know that I will").

The message of this book has been working on and in my life. But it's not enough to "hear" it–I need to "heed" it. I need to wave the white flag of surrender and say, "Yes, Lord"–and then do what I know He wants me to do.

I've "preached myself under conviction" while writing on giving thanks in all things. I know there is a greater measure of obedience and surrender that needs to take place in my life before I can release this book with freedom and a "true heart."

The obvious answer is, "So wave the white flag!" Truthfully, I'm just not there yet. But I'm sharing this with you as a step in that direction. I know He is Lord and worthy of my wholehearted, glad surrender.

As I wrote this email, I debated over whether to send it. I knew it would make me accountable in a way I wouldn't have to face if I just kept these issues in my heart.

But I also knew that God pours grace on the humble. I knew that "walking in the light" by humbling ourselves and confessing our need before God and others ("roof off, walls down") is essential in the process of transformation. I felt I had to take the step of sending that email if I wanted to press into the victory and transformation God wanted in this area of my life.

"YES, LORD"

The next morning I went to church, praying as I entered the service that the Lord would anoint the worship leader and the pastor. When the worship leader came to the platform, he spoke briefly about the need to fall on Christ Jesus the Rock in brokenness, so that the Rock will not have to fall on us and crush us (see Luke 20:18). I felt like this man had been reading my email!

He went on to say that "falling on the Rock" means we must be willing to "change when He asks us to," and to "align ourselves with His will." By this point, it was as if I was the only one in that service and God was speaking directly to me. I could hardly breathe.

Over the next quarter hour, we sang one song after another about the cross of Christ and the sacrifice He paid for our sin. We listened to the reading of Isaiah 53 about how our sins (including my sin of whining) were placed on Christ on the cross.

Then our pastor took us to the Word in preparation for the observance of the Lord's Supper. I always look forward to celebrating Communion. But of all days. As I sat with my Bible on my lap opened to 1 Corinthians 11, my eyes kept going to the verses about how Jesus' body was broken for me–as He said "Yes" to all the will of the Father–and about the danger of partaking of the bread or cup of the Lord "in an unworthy manner," of being "guilty concerning the body and blood of the Lord" (v. 27). I knew this was no glib moment.

As the elements were passed one by one, I held first the wafer in my hand, then the juice. I sat in the presence of Christ with tears in my eyes, meditating on the cross and grieved by the thought of holding anything back from Him, in the light of His great sacrifice.

My heart was deeply convicted by His Spirit, but drawn by His grace. I confessed my pride and resistance and asked Him to forgive me. I thanked Him for what He had done for me at Calvary. I let His blood wash over my heart.

And in my heart I waved the white flag and said, "*Yes, Lord.* I am willing to go with You all the way on this journey of choosing gratitude. I don't want to be just 'grateful enough' to keep up appearances. By Your grace, I want to put the axe to the root of every vestige of complaining, and become a radically thankful woman."

In that holy moment, I worshiped.

I realize that sanctification is a life-long process. And I don't expect that years of habit patterns will be undone overnight. "Putting off" the old life of the flesh and "putting on" the new life of the Spirit takes intentionality, humility, time, and effort.

> *In my heart I waved the white flag and said, "Yes, Lord. I am willing to go with You all the way on this journey of choosing gratitude."*

But my heart is set on this journey. I'm making myself accountable to others who are committed to the process with me until, by His grace, gratitude becomes the "default setting" of my heart and my response to all of life.

Will you go there with me? He is worthy!

Growing in
Gratitude:

A 30-DAY DEVOTIONAL GUIDE

Every time I hear the word grace,
I am reminded that I must live a life, every day,
which reflects my gratitude to God.

CHARLES W. COLSON[1]

I've learned over the years—and have often been reminded while writing this book—that being a thankful person is a choice. If I fail to choose gratitude, by default, I choose ingratitude. And once allowed into my life, ingratitude brings with it a lot of other undesirable companions that only succeed in tearing things up, then walking off with my joy. To not choose gratitude—daily and deliberately—is more costly than most realize.

As you've read this book, I trust the Lord has quickened within you a desire to respond to and reflect His grace in a lifestyle of heart-felt, humble gratitude. But gratitude, like other Christian virtues and disciplines, doesn't just "happen." It requires intentional effort. That's why I believe *the pages that follow may be the most important and life-changing part of this book.*

I read a lot of good books that challenge and convict me regarding specific areas of my walk with God. But far too often, once I've finished the book, I return it to my library and pick up the next good book I want to read–*before* I've taken time to respond to what I've just read by repenting, obeying, and applying the truth of God's Word in the laboratory of life.

The Devil (who by the way is the supreme example of *in*gratitude!) doesn't mind if you read a book on choosing gratitude–as long as you don't let the truth work its way into your heart and change the way you think and live. As long as you don't actually start "choosing gratitude"!

So before you put this book down, I want to challenge you to put into practice what you've just read. And that's going to require more than a few hurried minutes. As I pointed out in the last chapter, developing new habits and spiritual disciplines takes time.

I know . . . you're insanely busy and you don't need one more thing to do, right?! Well, if you'll carve out the time and stay with me through this challenge, I'm confident you will be *grateful* you did!

In chapter 9, I encouraged you to set aside a 30-day period to concentrate on cultivating the attitude of gratitude. That's what I want to help you do in this final section. You'll need to set aside twenty to thirty minutes each day, preferably at a time and in a place where distractions will be minimal. (To keep this time from getting squeezed out of your already-full days, try adding it to your calendar, like any other appointment.)

Two things you'll want to have with you on this journey:

1. Pack your Bible. We can't set out on this devotional adventure without taking the Scripture along. Each day includes a passage to look up. Don't just skim through it. Savor it. Meditate on it. Ask the Holy Spirit to highlight words and phrases that can be invested in your memory bank. It will be *His* words—not mine—that will transform you into a grateful person.

2. Bring a journal. There's just not enough room in the pages of this book to keep track of what God will be doing in you as you progress. We've created a companion journal to help you get the most out of this section. Visit www.reviveourhearts.com/choosing gratitude, for more information. Of course, you can simply use a blank journal or notebook. Here are some suggestions for how to develop your personal "Gratitude Journal" over the next several weeks (and beyond):

- Record a key thought and any further insight you gain from each day's Scripture reading, in relation to thankfulness.

- Record your responses to questions and assignments throughout this 30-day devotional. This will include "gratitude lists" in several different categories.

- Write out prayers in response to your study and meditation.

- Each day, make a list of five things you're thankful for that day. As you look for things to include each day, you'll be amazed at how your eyes are opened to see His mercies that are "new every morning" (Lamentations 3:23).

- Jot down other Scriptures you come across that relate to the theme of gratitude and thanksgiving.

- Capture any additional insights the Lord shows you about
  gratitude as you make this a focus of your thinking. Record how
  you're doing as you seek to cultivate a grateful heart. Identify
  what the Lord shows you along the way–heart issues that need
  to be addressed, "triggers" to ingratitude that you need to
  watch out for, helps in becoming more grateful, consequences
  of ingratitude and blessings of gratitude, the impact of grateful people on those around them, etc.

There's no "right way" to do this! You may find it helpful to
organize your "Gratitude Journal" by these sections, or you may
simply want to start fresh each day and make entries in these and/or
other areas related to gratitude.

One more word: This 30-day guide includes a lot of practical
exercises designed to help you become a more thankful person.
But don't get so preoccupied with trying to answer every question,
complete every "assignment," and make every list that you miss
the heart of the matter. These are just suggestions. If you find a
particular question or project isn't helpful . . . move on to the next
one. The point is to let the Lord speak to you through His Word, and
to respond to Him in humility and obedience, as you seek to make
gratitude a way of life.

Okay, let's get started!

DAY 1: *Defined by Gratitude*

SCRIPTURE READING: *Colossians 3:12–17*

. . . .

We've said that "gratitude is learning to recognize and express appreciation for the benefits we have received from God and from others." Let's break down these components a bit further today:

To "recognize" what we receive each day, the eyes of our heart must be open and alert. This means constantly being on the lookout for blessings, making each day a treasure hunt. I have a friend who makes a habit of thanking the Lord for ten things every morning before he gets out of bed. He wants to start his day by focusing on the goodness of God, rather than whatever problems or challenges he may have to deal with that day.

To "express appreciation" means that what's in our heart needs to come out! It means being intentional about thanking God and others for the blessings that come our way. It also means frequent opportunities to invest back into those who are involved in our lives. It's our return gift to them–and to the Lord.

Being mindful of "the benefits we have received" helps squeeze bitterness and entitlement from our hearts, replacing negative, depressing thoughts with the realization that our loving Father has showered us with good things, and that even the "bad things" in our lives are "benefits," intended to make us more like Jesus.

Gratitude changes the way we start the day, spend the day, and look back on the day. It defines us as people who value our relationship with God and with those He's placed around us. By thanking Him and others throughout the day, we are expressing humility, realizing these "benefits" are all undeserved.

GRATITUDE IN ACTION

1. Overall, how would you rate your "Gratitude Quotient"? (If you're not sure—or you want to know how others would answer that question about you—ask a couple of people who live or work with you . . . people you know will be honest with you!) Check any of the following that apply:

    ☐ I look at the world through grateful eyes and consistently express my gratitude to God and others.

    ☐ I know I've been greatly blessed, but I don't often stop to actually express my gratitude to God and others.

    ☐ To be honest, I had not thought a lot about gratitude until reading this book. I've got a long way to go to develop a lifestyle of gratitude.

    ☐ I'm a whiner! I tend to focus on my problems and I frequently express them to others.

2. Write a prayer asking the Lord to cultivate in you a more grateful heart over these next thirty days. If you have realized that your "Gratitude Quotient" is not what it should be, confess your ungrateful spirit to the Lord. Ask Him to forgive you and to transform you by the power of His Spirit into a truly thankful person.

3. Write down and memorize the definition of gratitude at the beginning of today's reading and review it whenever you're feeling less than thankful about where you are and what's going on.

DAY 2: *Abounding in Thanksgiving*

SCRIPTURE READING: *Colossians 1:3, 12; 2:7; 3:15–17; 4:2*

Every chapter in Paul's letter to the Colossians has at least one reference to the attitude of gratitude. In your Bible, underline or circle the words "thank," "thanks," "thanksgiving," "thankful," and "thankfulness" in the verses above.

Paul makes it clear that being thankful is not optional. We learn about the source, the nature, the frequency, the object, and the scope of thankfulness, and we are introduced to its companions. Record in your journal as many insights about Christian gratitude as you can find, from these verses in Colossians.

The central theme of Colossians is *Christ*. He is exalted and worshiped for:

- His divine nature
- being the Creator and Sustainer of all things
- His preeminence over all creation and over all cosmic rulers and powers
- His redemptive, reconciling work on the cross
- defeating the powers of darkness
- being the Head of the church which is His body
- being the fulfillment and substance of Old Testament types and figures
- being the believer's life and our hope of glory
- and so much more!

As those who have "died" with Christ, "been buried with him in baptism," and "raised with him through faith," our joy and hope do not emanate from any earthly source or from our religious practices, but from *Him*.

Within the four chapters of this short epistle, Paul calls us to be: sexually pure, compassionate, kind, humble, meek, patient, forgiving, loving, peaceful, obedient, just, wise, gracious, and *thankful! Whew*—that's a tall order! But everything we are called to be and do as "Christians" flows out of who *Christ* is in us, and what He has already done on our behalf.

As Christ abounds in His infinite splendor and in His grace toward us, so as we walk by faith in Him, we have abundant motivation—and divine enabling—to live a life that is always "abounding in thanksgiving."

GRATITUDE IN ACTION

As is the case regarding every virtue and everything that is expected of us as children of God, true thankfulness is rooted and grounded in Christ and His gospel. It is generated by His life within us. Read through one or more of the following passages from Colossians, meditating on them, praying them back to God, and using them as a basis for giving thanks to Him (I've helped you get started on the first one):

- 1:12–14–*Oh Father, I am so grateful and joyfully give You thanks, because though I was in no way related to You and had no right to have any part in Your kingdom, by Your grace, You have made me fit (qualified) to be a recipient—along with others who belong to Your family—of the infinite riches of Your inheritance....*

- 1:15–22
- 2:9–15
- 3:1–11

DAY 3: *Let the Redeemed Say So*

SCRIPTURE READING: *Psalm 107:1–32*

The theme of Psalm 107 is stated in the first two verses:

> *Oh give thanks to the Lord, for he is good,*
> *for his steadfast love endures forever!*
> *Let the redeemed of the Lord say so,*
> *whom he has redeemed from trouble.*

This theme is followed by four "personal testimonies"–illustrations of those who have been redeemed by the Lord and have reason to give Him thanks. Each testimony includes a similar progression:

- Distress–the straits people found themselves in
- Desperate cry to the Lord for help
- Divine deliverance

The passage is punctuated by a response–a "thanksgiving chorus" that is repeated at the end of each testimony (vv. 8, 15, 21, 31). Write out the words to that chorus in your journal.

How often do you consciously thank the Lord for His steadfast mercy and love and His "wondrous works" in your life?

GRATITUDE IN ACTION

1. Write out your personal testimony of God's saving grace, following the progression found in Psalm 107.

- What was your life like before He redeemed you? (If you need help getting started, take a look at Ephesians 2:1-3.)

- How did God bring you to the end of yourself, to the place where you cried out to Him for mercy?

- What has changed in your life since He delivered you from your slavery to sin?

2. If you have additional time, write another brief testimony of a time *subsequent* to your initial salvation, when you were in distress, you cried out to the Lord, and He came to your rescue.

3. Now, reread the first two verses of Psalm 107 and the "chorus" that recurs throughout. Take time to thank the Lord for His steadfast love and His redeeming work in your life.

4. *"Let the redeemed of the Lord say so"* (v. 2). Share your story (*His* story) with someone else today. Tell them how grateful you are to the Lord for saving you—eternally, as well as daily.

DAY 4: *Another . . . and Another*

SCRIPTURE READING: *Psalm 103:1–5*

. . . .

I recently interviewed a woman for our *Revive Our Hearts* broadcast who has faithfully memorized and meditated on Scripture for more than fifty years. She talked about the many benefits she has received as a result of hiding God's Word in her heart.

I was amazed when she mentioned that she had never really been depressed. She explained that whenever she finds herself becoming a bit down or blue, she begins to quote Psalm 103. At that point in the interview she proceeded to recite the entire psalm–from memory, thoughtfully, with heartfelt expression.

It was a moving experience for all of us who were in the room listening. When she got to the end of the passage, there was a holy hush. The first thought that went through my mind was, "How in the world could anyone ever be overwhelmed with depression, and how in the world could I ever give in to discouragement, if all these blessings are ours–and they are!"

As we recognize and identify the specific blessings we have received from God and from others, we discover countless reasons for expressing gratitude. The psalmist took time to bless the Lord for specific benefits–he didn't want to forget even one of them! As you open your heart to Him in prayer today, ask God to reveal to you just how great your "benefits package" really is.

Designate several pages in your journal or notebook for each of these two headings: "Gifts from God" and "Gifts from Others." Then start making a list of everything that comes to mind. As you try filling these in with personal examples, it's quite natural for your writing to stop and start, sometimes piling up faster than you can get the blessings down, sometimes drawing a blank about what to put next. So don't try forcing this into a one-time, ten-minute exercise. Keep adding to these lists as additional gifts come to mind over the next thirty days (and beyond!).

GRATITUDE IN ACTION

1. After you've written out a list of your blessings, take some time to walk through your list line by line, thanking God for each of these "benefits."

2. Read Psalm 103 aloud. Try memorizing and meditating on at least the first five verses over the next week or so.

DAY 5: *Digging Deeper*

SCRIPTURE READING: *Ephesians 5:15–21*

Since starting to catalogue some of your blessings yesterday, I hope you're becoming more alert to the many reasons you have to be grateful. But I'm reminded of that visual illustration about the jar filled with rocks. The speaker asks, "Would you say this jar is full?" Yes. "Is there any way it could hold any more?" No. But by continuing to add smaller pieces of rock and sand, we soon discover there was more room inside than we realized.

I remember hearing a friend tell how, while brushing his teeth one morning and meditating on one of the verses in today's reading (Ephesians 5:20), he was struck by the word "everything." He was reminded of the importance of thanking God for even those "little things" that we often overlook. It made him pause and be thankful for, well . . . his toothbrush. And his toothpaste. And, while he was at it, he thanked God for his teeth, for probably the first time in his life.

This may require another separate list from the ones you made yesterday, but it's definitely a category worth considering. Since everything is a gift from God (James 1:17), "everything" is something to be thankful for.

My friend told me he also asked himself: "If tomorrow's supply depended on today's thanksgiving, how much would I have tomorrow?" Something to think about!

GRATITUDE IN ACTION

1. What "little things" can you add to the gratitude lists you've started?

2. Some of the items on your "everything" list will make you realize you've taken certain people in your life for granted. Say thank you today in some way.

DAY 6: *Top Ten*

SCRIPTURE READING: *Romans 11:33–36*

. . . .

Robertson McQuilkin, former president of Columbia International University, tells of a time when, following his wife's diagnosis with Alzheimer's and the death of his eldest son, he retreated alone to a mountain hideaway, trying to reorient his heart and recapture a love for God that had slowly evaporated in the heat of personal, tragic loss.

It certainly didn't happen in the first five minutes, but after a day devoted to prayer and fasting, he began writing God a love letter, enumerating the gifts he had received from the Lord's hand, worshiping Him with pen and paper. In this season of revival, he identified ten particular blessings from God that just absolutely exceeded his imagination, things he could hardly find words to express how invaluable they were, how impossible life would be without them.

I like that. In fact, I encourage you to flip back through the lists you've been making the last few days and choose a top ten or so–a highlight reel of spiritual blessings that are so big, you could never generate enough gratitude to express what they mean to you and what they tell you about your Savior.

See if like Robertson McQuilkin you find your heart for God renewed by what he called "the reflex action of thanksgiving. My love flamed up from the dying embers, and my spirit soared. I discovered that ingratitude impoverishes–but that a heavy heart lifts on the wings of praise."[2]

GRATITUDE IN ACTION

Since a whole lifetime isn't enough to say thanks for these blessings, the next time your mind is troubled by sad or worrisome thoughts, pull out your top ten and consciously transfer your focus from whatever is weighing you down, and start giving thanks for the things on your list.

DAY 7: *Healing Gratitude . . . Say It Loud, Say It Clear*

SCRIPTURE READING: *Luke 17:11–15*

. . . .

W e talked in chapter 3 about Jesus' healing of the ten lepers, but notice a few more things that distinguished the one who returned to say "Thank you" to Jesus:

First, he came loudly. This was no private matter, nor was it a quiet one-on-one conversation with Jesus off in a corner somewhere. "One of them, when he saw that he was healed, turned back, *praising God with a loud voice*" (Luke 17:15). This man just couldn't contain his gratitude. This occasion called for an unrestrained, extreme, public display of thanks.

Oh, for such a grateful spirit as we see in this man. May the volume of our gratitude be cranked high not only when we're asking for help (as all ten of the lepers had done) but also when acknowledging our Helper. May our giving of thanks be as obvious and expressive as our sharing of needs!

I think of my dad, whose frequent response I mentioned earlier– "I'm doing *better than I deserve.*" I think of my dear friend "Mom Johnson," now in heaven after living a long earthly life of ninety-two years, who would often say, "I have more blessings than problems." I think of the most buoyant, approachable people I know–the ones I love spending time with, who bless and enrich my life whenever I am around them. It's not that they have the fewest problems, or the cleanest histories, or the most obvious reasons for happiness. They're simply the ones who are "loudest" about giving thanks, who are not always reciting a long list of problems, complaints, and criticisms but who choose to be grateful. They know they've already been given more than life could ever cost them. The Lord keeps them full despite the world's best attempts at depleting them. And they don't mind telling you about it.

I want to be one of those people, don't you?

Second, he came close. We never get any closer to Jesus than when we come with humble gratitude. The ten lepers who first met Jesus "stood at a distance" (v. 12)–lepers were ceremonially defiled and were not allowed to come close to those who were "clean." The healed leper who "fell on his face at Jesus' feet, giving him thanks" (v. 16) was the only one of the ten who ever got close to Jesus. Gratitude places us in close proximity to Christ, where we experience the fullness of His redeeming power and enjoy the blessing of His presence.

Third, he came from a distance. "He was a Samaritan" (v. 16). Unlike some of us who can't remember a time when we weren't at least somewhat aware of God's presence and power, this man had never known the true God until Jesus came into his world and transformed his life. After being separated from Jesus by a religious, cultural, and physical gulf, he loved what he saw in Jesus–up close and personal. Do you love what you see in Jesus? Gratitude will help bridge the distance and draw you close to Jesus.

Think today, not only about what you have to be grateful for, but about the blessings we receive when we take time to stop and express our gratitude to God and others.

GRATITUDE IN ACTION

Look for an opportunity today to thank the Lord for what He has done in your life–aloud, and in the presence of others. And don't whisper your prayer–speak up! You may feel a bit awkward if you're not accustomed to praise Him in this way. But think about how you express yourself when you are enthused or earnest about something in another realm of your life—say, being surprised with an engagement ring, receiving a promotion at work, or your kid's soccer game.

The point isn't to try to "stir up" vociferous praise—we don't have to speak loudly for God to hear us. But it makes sense that a true awareness of our hopeless, helpless condition apart from Him, coupled with His transforming grace and deliverance in our lives should evoke something more than muttered thanks!

DAY 8: *Gratitude and Humility*

Members of the Masai tribe in West Africa understand that gratitude and humility go hand in hand. When they want to say "Thank you," they touch their forehead down to the ground and say, literally, "My head is in the dirt."

Another African tribe expresses gratitude in a similar way by saying, "I sit on the ground before you." When someone wants to make his gratitude known, he goes and just sits quietly for a period of time in front of the hut of the person to whom he is grateful.

One of the fundamental qualities invariably found in a grateful person is *humility*. Gratitude is the overflow of a humble heart, just as surely as an ungrateful, complaining spirit flows out of a proud heart.

Proud people are wrapped up in themselves. They think much of themselves and little of others. If people or circumstances don't please or suit them, they are prone to whine or become resentful. Today's reading reminds us that "God opposes the proud"–the concept is that He stiff-arms them, He keeps them at a distance, He "sets Himself in battle array" against them.

But when we choose to "humble ourselves," as we are exhorted in James 4, God draws near to us and pours His grace into our lives. His Spirit does a cleansing, purifying work in our hearts, gives us victory over the noisy, demanding tyrant of self, and enables us to be thankful people, even in the midst of challenging circumstances.

Humble people are wrapped up in Christ. A humble person thinks much of God and others, and little, if at all, of himself. He recognizes that anything he has is better than he deserves. He does not feel anyone owes him anything. He does not feel entitled to have more, or for life to be easy, or for everyone to love him and treat him well. He is grateful for the least little kindness that is extended to him, knowing it is more than he deserves.

GRATITUDE IN ACTION

1. Make a list of anything you can recall "whining" about recently. Include things like frustrating people, annoying circumstances, wanting something you couldn't get (e.g., an uninterrupted nap), or having something you wished you didn't have (e.g., a cold). How does your complaining manifest a spirit of pride, entitlement, and expectations?

2. Sit quietly before the Lord for a time today and say, "I sit on the ground before You." You may even want to literally bow your head down to the ground as you come into His presence, as an expression of your desire to humble yourself before Him. Confess any pride that has shown itself in complaining, irritability, anger, or resentment, rather than giving of thanks. Humbly tell Him that you don't deserve any of His favor, and give Him thanks for any specific recent blessings He brings to mind—including those situations you have complained about! (If a circumstance involves something sinful or evil, ask how He might want to use it in your life to make you more like Jesus.)

DAY 9: *Gratitude and Generosity*

SCRIPTURE READING: *2 Corinthians 9:6–15*

. . . .

Where gratitude grows, you will generally find generosity flourishing as well. Yet, generosity is a most unnatural quality if ever there was one. I mean, here we stand today, in an age as risky, volatile, and dangerous as any other in memory, where conventional wisdom declares this is no time to be loose with our money and other resources. The financial commentators tell us what our hearts were already thinking: Protect what you can, because tomorrow could all be chaos.

Yet Paul expressed a surprising lack of concern for economic indicators when he advised the Corinthian church to let generosity be among the most notable expressions of their gratitude. His trust in God's supply was so strong, he treated as a "given" the fact that the church would "be enriched in every way to be generous in every way, which through us will produce thanksgiving to God" (v. 11). "God is able to make all grace abound to you, so that having all sufficiency in all things at all times, you may abound in every good work" (v. 8). In all things. At all times. Even these times.

Grateful people are generous people. Those who have "freely . . . received," are motivated to "freely give" (Matthew 10:8 NKJV).

GRATITUDE IN ACTION

1. Why do gratitude and generosity go hand in hand? Can we truly be defined by one without practicing the other?

2. What act(s) of generosity might gratitude be motivating you toward today? Ask God for wisdom and faith, then follow through on the promptings of His Spirit in relation to your giving.

DAY 10: *Invisible Blessings*

SCRIPTURE READING: *1 Corinthians 2:6–11*

· ·

Scottish minister Alexander Whyte was known for his uplifting prayers in the pulpit. He always found something for which to be grateful. But one Sunday morning, the weather was so dank and gloomy that the church members said among themselves, "Certainly the preacher won't think of anything to thank the Lord for on such a wretched day." Much to their surprise, however, Whyte stepped to the pulpit that dreary morning and began by praying, "We thank Thee, Lord, that it is not always like this."[3]

There are blessings in your life and mine that "no eye has seen, nor ear heard" (v. 9)–blessings that only show themselves by not showing up. Today, try listing as many of these things to be grateful for as you can think of.

For example, think of the miles you've driven without getting a flat tire. Think of the big tree out front that's never dropped a damaging limb on your house. Think of a destructive sin or habit the Lord has kept you from being tempted by. Perhaps you're hobbled by a medical problem or two, but think of a dozen you've never experienced.

Look at all the benefits on your growing list of gratitude-inducers, and by backing them into reverse like this, you'll find your blessings multiplying at an amazing rate.

GRATITUDE IN ACTION

Gratitude can (and should) lead us to intercession. A good prayer starter is to ask God to remind you of those who *do* suffer from some of the things He's spared you from. Lift these people up to Him today.

DAY 11: *The Greatest Gift of All*

SCRIPTURE READING: *Romans 5:1–11*

. . . .

If you're a Christian, the best thing that's ever happened to you is being saved from sure destruction for your sins and ushered into the family of God, beginning now and continuing for all eternity. Sit and ponder that reality for a while.

Sadly, time tends to dull our appreciation of the magnificent, sacrificial work of Christ on our behalf. Life gets so busy and complicated, we can go for weeks–or longer–without being swept away by the magnitude of our salvation.

One of my friends paraphrases the well-known memory verse of Romans 5:8 this way: "God demonstrated His love toward us in this: while we were in open, hostile rebellion toward Him, having no interest in Him–not only that but actively despising Him and all that He stands for–Christ died for us." How can we not be inexpressibly thankful? But praise God, gratitude can reopen the wonder to us, throwing back the dingy curtains of complacency until the full light of His grace and glory come streaming through.

GRATITUDE IN ACTION

The salvation we have in Christ is a "many-splendored thing," a diamond with countless brilliant facets. What spiritual blessings in today's Scripture reading need to be added to your list of "Gifts from God"?

DAY 12: *Gratitude You Can Feel*

SCRIPTURE READING: *3 John 1–4*

· ·

Numerous secular studies and research projects attest to the health benefits of the attitude of gratitude. The Research Project on Gratitude and Thanksgiving, conducted by two psychologists, broke several hundred people into three groups and required each person to keep a daily diary. The first group simply recorded events that occurred through the day. The second group was asked to journal negative experiences. The final group made a list each day of things for which they were grateful. The gratitude group reported greater levels of alertness and energy, exercised more frequently, and experienced less depression and stress.[4] From better sleep to fewer medical symptoms, gratitude just seems to satisfy.

The apostle John says to his beloved sons and brothers in Christ, "I pray that all may go well with you and that you may be in good health, as it goes well with your soul" (v.2). He's right—there's something physically strengthening and sustaining about being joyful in the Lord and grateful for His blessings. While living a godly life does not guarantee physical health, a healthy (spiritual) heart can do much to enhance our physical and emotional well-being. What are some reasons you think that might be the case?

GRATITUDE IN ACTION

We've been on this gratitude journey for more than ten days now. What differences have you noticed in your overall wellness and outlook? Add these "benefits" to your journal.

DAY 13: *Gratitude from Ground Zero*

SCRIPTURE READING: *Psalm 43:1–5*

....

The Psalms are a good place to camp out if your heart's desire is to be grateful–though not because they're filled with nothing but happy, upbeat sentiments. It surprises many who embark on a journey of the Psalms to find that they vibrate with every emotion known to man. They speak of back-breaking pressures, deep valleys of depression, times when life barely seems worth living. And yet, as we see in today's reading, the Psalms reveal that the only ultimate answer to trouble, grief, pain, and loss is a constant returning to God in worship and gratitude. Every other semisolution proves empty and short-lived, incapable of infusing real hope into life's unbearable situations.

"Why are you cast down, O my soul, and why are you in turmoil within me? Hope in God; for I shall again praise him, my salvation and my God" (Psalm 43:5). "My flesh and my heart may fail, but God is the strength of my heart and my portion forever" (73:26). "For his anger is but for a moment, and his favor is for a lifetime. Weeping may tarry for the night, but joy comes in the morning" (30:5).

Your heart may be crying out, "Oh God, let it be morning!" Keep hoping in Him until the day finally dawns. Even in the darkest night, you can still experience His peace and rest, knowing that the joy of morning is ahead. Resolve not to let your joy level be determined by the presence or absence of storms, but by the presence of God. Choose to be joyful in Him today.

GRATITUDE IN ACTION

Choose a few psalms–even if only at random–to read throughout the day today (aloud if possible). See if they don't cause praise and thanks to well up in your heart.

DAY 14: *Gratitude on the Run*

SCRIPTURE READING: *Psalm 56*

. . . .

Psalm 56 is a hymn of praise and trust, of confidence and strength, of worship and gratitude. If your Bible includes inscriptions at the beginning of selected Psalms, though, you'll notice that this particular one was written in far less than ideal circumstances.

David was on the run from King Saul, and when spotted and seized by the Philistines in the city of Gath, he had faked insanity to avoid being detained. This was definitely a desperate man in desperate straits.

Yet in the midst of intense, frightening hardship, he submitted himself to the Lord's protection, and found within this relationship the ability to say, "When I am afraid, I trust in you. . . . What can flesh do to me?" (vv. 3–4). He didn't deny the reality of what was happening to him, but he found reason to be grateful even for his sorrows, knowing that the Lord was catching every one of his tears in a bottle (v. 8).

The bottom line for David in this experience: "I will render thank offerings to you. For you have delivered my soul from death, yes, my feet from falling, that I may walk before God in the light of life" (vv. 12–13).

Perhaps it's hard for you to find much to be thankful for today. Perhaps all you can see is what's wrong, what hurts, and what others are doing to you. But look above your circumstances, beyond your fears, and ask God to show you what He's doing in the midst of them.

GRATITUDE IN ACTION

Look back through your list of blessings and benefits, adding any new ones that come to mind. Focus on the ones that give you the most comfort in crisis.

DAY 15: *Sacrifice of Thanksgiving*

SCRIPTURE READING: *Psalm 50:14–15, 23*

. . . .

As we saw in chapter 8–and as you know from your own experience–giving thanks sometimes requires a sacrifice. Plenty of occasions exist in life where being thankful is the last thing you feel like doing, where nothing seems good or gratitude-worthy.

The last few days' readings have been leading up to this, and though this is a hard task to undertake, I pray that you will open your heart to the Lord and choose to embrace it. Today, I'd like you to make a list of all the difficult things in your life right now. Spell them out, as detailed as you'd like to express them.

Then, when you get through writing, I want you to classify these not as burdens and impossibilities. Rather, I urge you to use this list as a prompt for giving thanks.

That assignment may seem strange–or impossible! We are not expected to thank God "*for*" things that are sinful. But we can give thanks "*in* everything," knowing that God is still God and He uses all things in this fallen world to accomplish His purposes, one of which is the sanctification of His children.

Yes, to give thanks as you consider the list before you will be a sacrifice. You probably won't *feel* like making this sacrifice. But it will be pleasing to the Lord. And what's more, His promise to those who make gratitude their practice is that He will "show [them] the salvation of God" (v. 23). When gratitude becomes your newly adopted attitude and lifestyle–even in the midst of pressures and problems–you will see His deliverance in new and amazing ways.

Begin to track the ways that God is using these circumstances in your life. Perhaps they are causing you to become more dependent on Him, or to call upon Him in prayer, or to exercise faith in His promises.

When we call upon our Lord "in the day of trouble" (v. 15), with minds set on glorifying Him, He does marvelous things in the midst of our pain and sorrow. Thank Him by faith that He can use each of these situations as a means to display His glory.

GRATITUDE IN ACTION

Pray over any painful situations and broken relationships on your list. Ask God for tailor-made grace and for wisdom regarding each one. Then, rather than complaining about them, ask Him to show you how to turn them into praises. Open your heart to receive them as opportunities for His grace to shine through.

DAY 16: *Sing and Give Thanks*

My mother was an exceptionally gifted, classically trained singer. I, on the other hand, apparently inherited my dad's genes in that area. By most anyone's standards, he had a poor singing voice. But he used the voice he had to sing praises aloud. He was not timid or self-conscious when he sang, and gave no indication of being concerned about what others thought! I am grateful for his example and have tried to emulate it.

Unlike most other religions, Christianity is a "singing" faith. The word "sing" occurs over one hundred times in the Bible—more than sixty of them in the book of Psalms alone. *Psalms* has appropriately been called the "hymn book of ancient Israel." The psalmists sometimes sang songs of lament and longing. But most often they sang songs of praise and thanks to God. Verses 4 and 12 in today's Scripture reading both tie singing and giving thanks together.

I've often pondered why Scripture places such emphasis on praising the Lord with singing, and why it is that all believers are commanded to sing to the Lord, regardless of their natural ability. There are a number of illustrations in Scripture of the powerful effect of praise through music. (For starters, try 2 Chronicles 20:21-23, where God gave a great victory to the Israelites after the choir held a praise service at the front of the troops marching into battle!)

There is no doubt that the Devil despises Godward praise. We have some reason to believe that at one time, before pride caused him to lose his position, he may have been one of the "worship leaders" in heaven and therefore is particularly repulsed and repelled when God's people praise Him with singing and musical instruments.

When I talk with a woman who is struggling with chronic discouragement or depression, I often ask two questions: (1) Are you memorizing Scripture? and (2) Are you singing to the Lord? I'm not suggesting these are magic "pills" that will make every emotional struggle go away, but I have found these two means of grace to be extremely effective at recalibrating my heart and restoring inner peace.

I have often experienced fresh springs of God's grace as I have exercised faith in singing to Him in praise and thanksgiving. At times, when I am deeply distraught or discouraged, I will open my hymnal and just begin to sing. Songs like "Leaning on the Everlasting Arms" or "'Tis So Sweet to Trust in Jesus" (all stanzas!). Occasionally I am crying so hard I can scarcely get the words out. But as I sing to the Lord, my heart and mind are re-tethered to His goodness and love, and invariably, the cloud begins to lift. In fact, I sing *until* the cloud lifts.

GRATITUDE IN ACTION

As today's reading exhorts us, *"Sing praises to the Lord . . . and give thanks to his holy name"* (v. 4)! Whether it's a cloudy or sunny day in your heart, sing! Right now, if possible. Put on a CD or your iPod headset and sing along with others, or just sing to Him on your own–the Lord will love your "joyful sound"!

Sing praise choruses that are familiar to you, or pull out a hymnal and sing some of those rich hymns by Charles Wesley, Isaac Watts, Fanny Crosby, or Frances Havergal, that we don't sing often enough anymore. (I've listed some of my favorite hymns on pages 225-26.) A friend recently shared with me that she has taken it upon herself to *memorize* hymns, so she can sing them as she goes about her housecleaning and other responsibilities. Great suggestion!

DAY 17: *Happiness Is . . .*

SCRIPTURE READING: *Proverbs 3:13–18*

. . . .

W e've spent a few days in the Psalms, letting gratitude continue to grow in us as we see God's people of old choose thanksgiving over bitterness.

Choosing to be grateful is a decision rooted in godly wisdom, a theme highlighted in the book of Proverbs. I've heard wisdom described as "skill in everyday living." And training our hearts to be grateful for the blessings of God that we experience is linked to our pursuit of godly wisdom in every area of our lives.

When the writer of Proverbs outlines the benefits of wisdom, he is also advertising the benefits of every other habit and discipline inspired by the Scriptures. And since the practice of being thankful is a basic characteristic of God's people, I believe these passages that call us to wise, godly living can appropriately be applied to the issue of gratitude as well.

That's why I really like what's implied in today's reading. It begins and ends with a word–"blessed"–that portrays the type of person God desires and enables us to be. Some translations of the Bible use a slightly different word that helps us better understand what God is offering us, what He promises to those who choose wisdom and gratitude, who choose to accept and believe that His ways are be desired above all others. That word is "happy."

For most people, *happiness* is tied to circumstances–to what is *happening* in their lives. For Christians, however, happiness or blessedness is not dependent on the weather, the stock market, or how our last haircut turned out. Real happiness–that unshakable sense of peace, contentment, and well-being–comes as we remind ourselves of the blessings we have in Christ, and then respond with thankfulness.

I want that kind of happiness, don't you? And apparently God wants it for us too. He wants us to experience the deep, inner happiness that is the lot of those who are completely satisfied with Christ.

So as we're seeking the Lord for grateful hearts, let's not be surprised to see ourselves smiling a little more than usual, being more easily contented, and happy with God and what He is accomplishing in us.

GRATITUDE IN ACTION

We've talked about being "loud" with our thanksgiving, being vocal about what God is doing. Check to be sure your countenance is also expressing a joyful, thankful heart.

DAY 18: *The High Cost of Grumbling*

SCRIPTURE READING: *1 Corinthians 10:1–13*

....

In today's reading, Paul reflects back on the children of Israel in the wilderness and identifies four specific sins they committed, all of which had dire consequences. What are those four sins?

- v. 7
- v. 8
- v. 9
- v. 10

All of these sins resulted in tragic outcomes. We can understand God punishing idolatry and sexual immorality. But it's sobering to realize that He includes the sin of "grumbling" (your translation may say "murmur" or "complain") with these other sins and takes them all seriously!

The sin referred to in 1 Corinthians 10:10 relates to incidents recorded in Numbers 11:1; 14:1–28; 16:11–35. Take a few moments to skim through these passages to give you some context.

Every time I read these Old Testament accounts, I am convicted of how my murmuring and complaining displeases the Lord (and how merciful He is not to judge me as He did the Israelites!).

Grumbling is the opposite of thankfulness. Like gratitude, it starts in the heart and expresses itself in our words. It grows out of the sin of discontentment–not being satisfied with what God has provided.

Philippians 2:14–15 says we are to "do *all* things without grumbling," and that when we are obedient in this matter, our lives shine the light of Christ into our dark world.

Are you guilty of the sin of grumbling? If so, confess that to the Lord; ask Him to forgive you and to grant you true repentance. Purpose in your heart to "put off" all complaining and to "put on" a heart of thankfulness.

GRATITUDE IN ACTION

Ask God to make you sensitive and alert to situations over the next twenty-four hours where your natural response would be to murmur or whine. Ask Him for grace to *give thanks* every time you're tempted to grumble. (If you have a pattern of complaining, it probably won't disappear in a day! This is one exercise you'll need to do intentionally day after day, until your "default response" has changed from grumbling to gratitude.)

DAY 19: *People Matter*

SCRIPTURE READING: *Romans 1:8; 1 Corinthians 1:4;*
Ephesians 1:15–16; Philippians 1:3–4; Colossians 1:3–4;
1 Thessalonians 1:2–3; 2 Thessalonians 1:3

....

The apostle Paul was a grateful man. That's because he never forgot where God found him. He never forgot how greatly he had sinned against the holiness and the law of God, and the church of Jesus Christ. And he never got over the wonder of the amazing grace of God that had reached down to him, undeserving as he was. His life is a great illustration of the principle we have seen that: "guilt + grace → gratitude."

When you read Paul's New Testament letters to various believers and churches, you can't help but notice his many expressions of gratitude for spiritual blessings lavished on those who are in Christ: the grace of God, the saving work of Christ, forgiveness of sin, the gift of the Spirit, the privilege of ministry–the list is lengthy.

If you took time to read the verses listed above, you also couldn't help but notice that Paul was thankful for *others*–especially for brothers and sisters in Christ, fellow servants, ministry partners. In his correspondence (and he was quite the letter writer), Paul didn't just leave it at generalized expressions of gratitude–he often took time to identify specific individuals for whom he was grateful and to let them know how much he appreciated their contribution to his life and ministry.

The most extensive such list is found in Romans 16:1–16. In fact, why not turn there now and read through that passage (you probably haven't meditated on this one for a while!). As you read, underline in your Bible or make a list in your journal of words or phrases that describe what Paul was grateful for in these believers in Rome.

Most of the names in this list–many of them hard to pronounce–represent people about whom we know little or nothing. From a human perspective, none of them attained the "position" or "importance" Paul had as an apostle. Why did Paul think it necessary, inspired by the Holy Spirit, to take valuable time and space to write this lengthy passage? I think one reason is that he saw these people as provisions of God's grace. And he knew no one is self-sufficient–we need each other and our lives are enriched and blessed by other like-hearted believers.

People matter to God. And they should matter to us. It's important to take time to recognize and express appreciation for the contributions that even little-known people make to His kingdom and to our lives.

Inspired by the example of the apostle Paul and others, I've tried to make it a point over the years to stop and take stock periodically of my "gratitude accounts"–to make sure they're "caught up," and to find meaningful ways to express gratitude for and to the people who have contributed to my life. I'm sure those expressions encourage the recipients. But they also provide a much-needed antidote in my own life to pride, independence, isolation, and self-reliance.

GRATITUDE IN ACTION

1. Make a list in your journal of individuals who have blessed or touched your life in some way. To help you get started . . . how about: the person who introduced you to Jesus, your parents, other family members, pastors, teachers, coaches, friends, co-workers, neighbors, authors, leaders of Christian ministries–you get the idea.

   As you write each name, ask yourself, "Have I ever thanked this person for the way God has used him/her in my life?" Put a checkmark next to each individual to whom you have expressed gratitude.

2. Begin the process of catching up on your "gratitude accounts." Don't try to tackle the whole list at once. Pick one for starters. In the next twenty-four hours, write a letter, make a call, compose an email–find a way to express your gratitude for that person's influence and impact in your life.* Then move to the next one . . . and the next . . . until you've expressed gratitude to each person on your list. By that time, there will undoubtedly be new people to add to the list! And–you can always start over again with the same list.

* Check out www.reviveourhearts.com/choosinggratitude to find some attractive note cards designed for this purpose.

DAY 20: *Gratitude at Home*

SCRIPTURE READING: *1 Timothy 5:8; 2 Timothy 1:3–5; 3:14–15*

....

It seems that it's often easier to express gratitude for and to people we hardly know, than for and to those in our own family. Maybe that's because we know our family members so well (and they know us!). Or it may be that we really do appreciate them, but we've come to take them for granted.

Godly character in every area of our lives will show up within the four walls of our homes. We can't say we love God if we don't manifest His love to our family members or if we allow bitterness to fester in our hearts toward them.

For the most part, we don't get to choose our family members, as we do our "friends." Yet we are called to love and care for those in our families, in spite of their personalities, their idiosyncrasies, or their character flaws. And that's not always easy!

Timothy had a godly mother and grandmother (not hard to be thankful for them). We don't know much about Timothy's father, but many Bible scholars believe that he was probably not a believer. He may or may not have been supportive of the faith of his wife and son. But it was no accident that Timothy grew up in the family he did. Though it was probably not an "ideal" home situation (what home situation is ideal?!), he still had much in his family for which to be grateful.

Regardless of your family heritage, it's important to realize that your relatives are not the result of "genetic chance," but that you have been placed into the family of God's sovereign choosing for you, and that He wants to use your family–rough edges and all–as a means to sanctify you and conform you into the likeness of His Son.

Embracing that truth will help you cultivate a grateful heart for those who make up your family.

GRATITUDE IN ACTION

1. Today, focus on expressing gratitude for and to your family members. In your journal, make a list of each member of your immediate family (mate, parents, children, siblings, etc.). Then next to each name write one quality about their life for which you are particularly grateful.

2. Take time to thank God for each member of the family He has given you. Then pick one or two individuals from your list to whom you can express gratitude today, in person, by phone, or with a note or email. You might want to start by saying something like this:

    Today, I thanked God for you. And I wanted to tell you how grateful I am that you are part of my family, and especially for this particular quality I see in your life . . .

(Note: You may want to express gratitude to a family member who has been especially difficult to love.)

DAY 21: *Family Matters*

SCRIPTURE READING: *Proverbs 21:2–9*

. . . .

If you were faithful to read the above passage, you can probably guess which verse I wanted to highlight: "It is better to live in a corner of the housetop than in a house shared with a quarrelsome wife" (v. 9). And, yes, I am serious about the dangers posed by tongues that are contentious, combative, and discontented.

But while heeding this as a warning, let's also turn it into a positive. If one of the blessings of gratitude is that it makes us generally happier people, it follows that gratitude makes those who live with us happier too.

Let the first halves of these proverbs become as desirable to you as the second halves are detestable: "The wisest of women builds her house, but folly with her own hands tears it down" (Proverbs 14:1). "A gentle tongue is a tree of life, but perverseness in it breaks the spirit" (15:4). "An excellent wife is the crown of her husband, but she who brings shame is like rottenness in his bones" (12:4).

The restorative power of a grateful heart and tongue is more potent than we can imagine, as is the destructive potential of being bitter and difficult to live with. "Gracious words are like a honeycomb, sweetness to the soul and health to the body" (Proverbs 16:24). Let's make sure our words have that kind of effect.

GRATITUDE IN ACTION

Ask God to guard your heart—and your tongue—today. Anytime you hear yourself saying words that are contentious, complaining, or critical, rather than gracious, gentle, and godly . . . stop. Ask Him to forgive you. And seek forgiveness from those to whom—or in whose presence—you spoke.

DAY 22: *Glad for What We Have*

Gratitude and contentment are not the same thing, but they are close enough cousins that it's helpful to see them working together in our hearts. This passage from the Proverbs is one that unites them in a most compelling way.

You may have heard some preachers and teachers leave the impression that God intends for every Christian to be materially rich. Others, though, swing the pendulum too far the other way, proudly wearing poverty like a cloak of self-righteous sainthood. Today's proverb puts a proper perspective on the whole thing.

The Word is teaching us to focus less on our climb up or down the economic ladder, and more on being grateful for where we are—not only because to do otherwise would be sinful and proud, but also because we don't know what the Lord may be saving us from by not giving us everything we might want. Even if we possess much less than others have, if our hearts are full of gratitude, neither money nor the lack of it can shake our contented dependence on God.

GRATITUDE IN ACTION

Money isn't everything, but our desire for it and the things it buys can certainly squash the vibrancy of our gratitude. Ask the Lord to show you if there is any root of discontentment or "love of money" in your heart. Ask Him to provide just what He knows you need—enough to keep you from being tempted to sin to get your needs met, but not so much that you no longer need to rely on Him as your Provider. Take some time to thank Him for His practical, material provision in your life today.

DAY 23: *Gratitude Is Always Enough*

SCRIPTURE READING: *1 Timothy 6:6–10*

....

Andrew Carnegie, the wealthy industrialist whose fortune rivaled that of any other contemporary at the time of his death in 1919, left a million dollars to one of his relatives, who in return became angry and bitter toward his generous benefactor because Mr. Carnegie had also left $365 million to charitable causes.

On its face, we can hardly believe this. How can a person have a million reasons to be grateful yet find it *hundreds* of millions short of being adequate? But don't we all possess some sense of entitlement toward God? How often does our expectation or demand for "more," tower over the plenty we already possess?

That's because we forget that God doesn't owe us anything. We are debtors. *We* are the ones who owe. We think we deserve more (or different or better) than we have, and therefore we forget or minimize the blessings God has already given and continues to give. Not content with food, clothing, and a roof over our heads, we whine if we don't have a certain kind of house, a certain kind of car, a certain kind of job, a certain kind of marriage, and certain kinds of friends living in a certain kind of neighborhood and income bracket.

The fact is, we're often not so different than Carnegie's ungrateful beneficiary. It's time we let gratitude be our ticket to freedom. It's true–being grateful can lead us to a place of simple satisfaction.

GRATITUDE IN ACTION

What kinds of "wants" are you defining as "needs"? Ask God to show you any ways you may have become blinded to His grace. Highlight them. Confess them. And trade them in on the bounty God promises to the grateful.

DAY 24: *A Woman after God's Heart*

SCRIPTURE READING: *Ruth 2:1–13*

S peaking of good examples to follow, the biblical account of Ruth is one that I find particularly moving and instructive every time I read it. Ruth was a woman with a humble heart–a trait we've identified as a companion virtue of gratitude. She didn't claim her rights. She didn't insist that Boaz provide her a living by letting her glean in his fields. And because she relinquished her demands for certain expectations, she was able to be genuinely thankful when she actually did receive the blessing of his generosity. Verses 10 and 13 are not a show of false flattery but the expressions of a heart operating out of humble gratitude.

Too many of us live with a chip on our shoulder, as if the world owes us something. "You ought to do this for me. You ought to serve me. You ought to meet my needs." But the humble heart–the grateful heart–says, "I don't deserve this, and it's an amazing act of grace that you should minister to my needs."

I once journaled the following prayer after meditating on Ruth's story: "O God, please take me back to see where You found me and where I would be today apart from You. Please strip me of my proud, demanding ways and clothe me in meekness, humility, and gratitude. Empty me of myself and fill me with the sweet, gracious nature of Jesus Christ."

Ruth just went out to serve with a humble, thankful heart. And as a result, God made sure her needs were met. He'll do the same for you.

GRATITUDE IN ACTION

1. Who do you know who consistently exhibits a grateful spirit? What is it about them that makes them so remarkable? What can you learn from their example?

2. Journal your own prayer in response to Ruth's example. Ask God to help you exemplify Ruth's kind of character.

DAY 25: *Thanksgiving Day*

SCRIPTURE READING: *Deuteronomy 8:1–10*

Historians have differing perspectives in relation to the first Thanksgiving celebrations in America. But there are some details we know for sure to be true. We know that the Pilgrims' journey from Holland to England to the New World was frightfully difficult, with sickness and storms their frequent visitors on the arduous, weeks-long voyage. We know that once they arrived, the task of carving dwellings out of the forest quick enough to hold back the advancing effects of winter was a losing race against time. Nearly half of those who made the trip didn't survive the stay. The Pilgrims certainly built more graves than huts.

And yet with sheer survival the order of each day, and with fears for their families an all-consuming worry, their writings and recorded history are filled with demonstrations and attitudes of thanksgiving.

Each Sunday–from the first landing of the *Mayflower* through the subsequent years of their little colony, in lean times as well as relatively plentiful–they gathered for prayer, meditation, the singing of hymns, and a sermon. It was their regular practice to stop and give thanks to God at the outset of each week.

Though having to be restricted to half-rations when their stores of crops proved insufficient for the first, long winters, William Bradford commented that they were learning by experience "the truth of the word in Deuteronomy 8:3–that man lives not by bread alone, but by every word that proceeds out of the mouth of the Lord."[5]

And when the years began slowly bringing a renewed abundance of harvests, rather than telling God they could manage just fine by themselves from here on, Edward Winslow wrote, "Having these

many signs of God's favor and [acceptance], we thought it would
be a great ingratitude if secretly we should content ourselves with
private thanksgiving. . . . Therefore, another solemn day [referring
back to a day of prayer and fasting they had observed earlier in the
summer] was set apart and appointed for that end; wherein we
returned glory, honor, and praise, with all thankfulness to our God
who dealt so graciously with us."[6]

What a wonderful example those early Pilgrims provide of choosing gratitude in times of plenty and times of want!

GRATITUDE IN ACTION

Use your prayer time today to think back over the history of God's
faithfulness in your life, your family, and your church. Make a list
of desperate situations or seasons when you have witnessed His
providential protection and provision.

DAY 26: *A Call to Gratitude*

SCRIPTURE READING: *Ezra 3:8–13*

. . . .

On October 3, 1863, at the height of the Civil War, President Abraham Lincoln issued a Proclamation of Thanksgiving, calling the nation to observe a "day of Thanksgiving and Praise." This proclamation eventually led to the establishing of our national day of Thanksgiving.

The document began by listing multiple blessings the nation had experienced through the course of the year, even in the midst of a severe conflict. It called the American people to recognize the Source of those blessings and to respond collectively to the Giver in gratitude, repentance, and intercession. Here's an excerpt:

> No human counsel hath devised nor hath any mortal hand worked out these great things. They are the gracious gifts of the Most High God, who, while dealing with us in anger for our sins, hath nevertheless remembered mercy.

> It has seemed to me fit and proper that they should be solemnly, reverently and gratefully acknowledged as with one heart and one voice by the whole American People. I do therefore invite my fellow citizens in every part of the United States . . . to set apart and observe the last Thursday of November next, as a day of Thanksgiving and Praise to our beneficent Father who dwelleth in the Heavens.

> And I recommend to them that . . . they do also, with humble penitence for our national perverseness and disobedience . . . fervently implore the interposition of the Almighty Hand to

heal the wounds of the nation and to restore it as soon as may
be consistent with the Divine purposes to the full enjoyment of
peace, harmony, tranquillity and Union.

Set against a background of divisive conflict, our nation's leader
in the 1860s was humble enough to know that our nation needed
God and needed to be grateful. This kind of heart is no less needed
in our nation today than it was then.

The call to gratitude goes beyond the church and into every
avenue of life. Pray today for a humble, grateful, repentant spirit to
be birthed in our own hearts, and among our leaders at every level.

GRATITUDE IN ACTION

1. You may not consider yourself to be much of a writer. That's
okay. But today I want you to try crafting your own declaration of
thanksgiving. Use some of the insights the Lord has been growing
in you these last few weeks. Incorporate some of the Scriptures
that have particularly touched you. And dedicate your life to what
these words of yours are saying. Make this your own declaration of
thanksgiving in your heart and home.

2. It's not enough to keep this to yourself. Share what you've written
with your family or a close friend. Post it on Facebook, send an
email to your friends. Be an igniter of gratitude by encouraging
those you love and care about to cultivate a thankful heart.

DAY 27: *Progress Report*

SCRIPTURE READING: *1 Timothy 4:11–16*

We're nearing the end of our month-long journey into gratitude. To help you measure what kind of effect this experience is having on your life, take a little quiz today to see where you're growing and where you still need work. Try answering these questions candidly in your journal—not just yes or no, but with supporting details that come to mind:

1. Do I often complain about my circumstances, feeling like I deserve better?

2. Do others hear me voice more complaints and negative comments than words of gratitude about the typical events of daily life?

3. Would others describe me as a thankful person?

4. What evidence is there that I have a grateful or an ungrateful spirit?

5. How often do I begin statements with these words: "I am so thankful that . . ."?

6. Do I more frequently display a pessimistic, negative outlook or a positive, grateful perspective?

7. Am I reserved or eager when it comes to expressing appreciation to others?

8. My most recent expression of gratitude was . . .

GRATITUDE IN ACTION

As I have shared, through the course of writing this book, God has done a fresh work in my own heart in the area of gratitude. But I had to be willing to humble myself, confess my need, and ask for prayer, help, and accountability from those close to me. Remember, our hearts cannot change apart from His grace giving us the desire and the power to please Him. And God pours out His grace on the humble.

If you haven't done so already, consider taking this gratitude challenge into an accountability setting, letting others help you stay true to your commitment, while being there to offer your support to them as well.

DAY 28: *Gratitude Accounts*

SCRIPTURE READING: *Philippians 1:3–11*

....

I have found that anything I fail to plan into my day usually doesn't get done. If I don't start the morning realizing that some particular thing is a priority, my mind isn't likely to remember it once the everyday pressures start squeezing everything else out of their way.

If expressing gratitude is to become a way of life for us, we can't treat it as an optional exercise. If it never gets beyond our wish list, if it nestles down with all the other nice things we hope to get around to someday, the "someday" of gratitude will never roll around on our calendars. It will remain a sweet intention, but not a consistent practice.

So I want to encourage you to think of gratitude as being a debt you owe, the same way you're called upon to pay your monthly bills. I'd like to see you open a section in your journal that's designated for "Gratitude Accounts," specific listings of individuals to whom you owe a debt of thanks.

By doing this, you can make it a point today to make a phone call just to thank a friend for the way she's shown her concern for you during a difficult time. You'll be reminded that when you see a certain person at the gym this afternoon, you need to be sure to thank her for helping you stay true to your fitness goals. When the Lord opens a window of opportunity for you to jot a quick thank-you note this evening, you'll have a ready-made list of people to choose from.

We all have gratitude accounts. There just aren't many of us who keep them paid up. Make sure you're becoming the type of person who stays current on your bill.

GRATITUDE IN ACTION

Who needs to be added to your Gratitude Account? What gratitude debt do you need to pay *today*?

DAY 29: *Growing Grateful Children*

SCRIPTURE READING: *Deuteronomy 6:1–12*

Like anything that God is growing in us, His intention in helping us become more like Christ is not merely to benefit ourselves but to help us inspire the same in others, to show them the blessings inherent in trusting the Lord.

If you have been blessed with children, you know that gratitude –like most every other character trait–doesn't come naturally for them. But few things are more remarkable (and unusual) in children today than when they're known for their thankful, contented spirit. It is a quality worth every ounce of effort we make to instill it in them.

And while teaching and instruction have their place in grow- ing gratitude in our kids, the best teacher of all (of course) is our example. Do your children hear you thank your husband when he tackles a home repair job or gets the car lubed? Do they hear you express gratitude to the Lord and to others for both little and big things throughout the day? Do you tell them how grateful you are for their dad, for your church and your pastor, for their teachers, for the house the Lord has provided for your family, for good health, and for God's abundant blessings to your family? Conversely, do they hear you grumble when your husband delays dinner by needing to see one extra client or when you get a flat tire or the sun doesn't come out for a week?

Gratitude joins many other important virtues that are more effectively caught than taught. How contagious are you, especially at home?

GRATITUDE IN ACTION

1. Sit down and talk with your children about the high value God places on gratitude. Tell them how they're going to start seeing some "gratitudinal" changes in you.

2. You may not have children of your own. Who has God placed in your sphere of influence? What are you teaching them about gratitude by your lifestyle?

DAY 30: *Pressing on in Gratitude*

SCRIPTURE READING: *Galatians 5:16–24*

· ·

As we begin to launch out on a new lifestyle of gratitude, let's use today to set some goals for what we want God to accomplish in our hearts, being specific about the ways we intend to practice ongoing thankfulness.

For example, if you want to become more deliberate about writing thank-you notes, how many would you like send in a typical week or month? What Scriptures do you plan to memorize and meditate on in relation to thankfulness? Whom will you ask to hold you accountable for specific areas where you need to grow in the grace of gratitude?

Remember, these are not added burdens tacked on to further complicate your day and put a drain on your time. As believers, we've been released from the oppressive demands of the law. As those who are in Christ, we are free to pursue godly living as our glad response to grace received. And we are enabled by the power of His Spirit to obey His will from our hearts. Resist every attempt of the Enemy to enslave you, even to good habits and activities.

As you grow in gratitude, you will be so blessed by its reward and spiritual significance that you won't feel as though it's an effort to accomplish it. Whatever mechanics it requires to get it up and running will soon fall away to the freedom of pursuing it with passion.

Are you ready to experience the life-changing power of Christian gratitude? Then let the Lord help you decide what your next steps should be.

GRATITUDE IN ACTION

1. Be bold and exercise faith, but don't be afraid to take short strides as you make this your manner of living. Do try, though, to be as specific as you can in plotting your gratitude plan.

2. Write a simple prayer, expressing to the Lord your desire to develop a radically grateful lifestyle. Thank Him for His supernatural grace that will enable you to "abound in thanksgiving."

A Grateful
Prayer

I am so glad that you've joined me in this journey toward a lifestyle of gratitude–a lifestyle I pray you'll practice for the rest of your life, as you prepare to spend eternity giving thanks! In closing our time together, I'd like to lift a prayer to the Lord, asking Him to bless us in the continued pursuit of this calling to be thankful people.

Father, we are astounded at the depths to which You have reached down to redeem us. We don't have language to describe the amazing grace You continue to lavish upon us with the dawn of each new day. And now, at the first light of what we pray will be a new day in our relationship with You and others, we ask Your favor and blessing in the living of it. We need Your help, for apart from the redeeming, sanctifying work of Christ for us and in us, we cannot begin to please You or to live in accord with Your Word.

I pray for myself and for my dear friends who have walked with me through these pages. We have heard Your Spirit calling us to reject the bitter clutches of ingratitude and to embrace the manifold joys of thanks-giving. May Your call continue to resonate in our hearts. May the multitude of Your blessings never be lost on us but rather reflected back as praises, poured like fuel onto our worship.

When the Enemy comes against us, when emotions or life experiences insist that joyful gratitude isn't possible, may You visit us with the life-giving strength of Your presence. When others misunderstand us or tell us we're living in denial, may we find sweet justification for our joy in the precepts of Your Word.

Father, we embark on this new chapter with great anticipation, sure of many lives that You intend to touch through our obedience, and also sure of many trials that You will transform into opportunities to bless us. Our desire is to reflect Your faithfulness, goodness, and grace through our grateful hearts and words. May You be glorified in us, in our gratitude.

We pray in the blessed name of our Savior, Jesus Christ, to whom we owe everything.

And one more thing—now and forever: Thank You, Lord.

Hymns of
Gratitude

Singing hymns to the Lord has been a wonderful aid in my personal worship and thanks-giving. Here are some I've found myself returning to repeatedly over the years. The words and music to these hymns can be found in many hymnals (if you don't own one, I'd encourage you to purchase one), as well as at www.cyberhymnal.com.

All the Way My Savior Leads Me (Fanny Crosby)

And Can It Be That I Should Gain (Charles Wesley)

Be Still, My Soul (Katharina von Schlegel)

Be Thou My Vision (Attributed to Dallan Forgaill)

Beneath the Cross of Jesus (Elizabeth Clephane)

Calvary Covers It All (Mrs. Walter G. Taylor)

Children of the Heavenly Father (Karolina W. Sandell-Berg)

Day by Day (Karolina W. Sandell-Berg)

Fairest Lord Jesus (*Münster Gesangbuch)*

Great Is Thy Faithfulness (Thomas O. Chisholm)

Guide Me, O Thou Great Jehovah (William Williams)

He Hideth My Soul (Fanny Crosby)

He Leadeth Me (Joseph H. Gilmore)

How Firm a Foundation (John Rippon)

How Sweet the Name of Jesus Sounds (John Newton)

I Am His, and He Is Mine (George W. Robinson)

It Is Well with My Soul (Horatio Spafford)

Jesus, I Am Resting, Resting (Jean Pigott)

Jesus Is All the World to Me (Will L. Thompson)

Jesus, Lover of My Soul (Charles Wesley)

Jesus Paid It All (Elvina M. Hall)

Jesus, the Very Thought of Thee (Bernard of Clairvaux)

Jesus! What a Friend for Sinners! (J. Wilbur Chapman)

Join All the Glorious Names (Isaac Watts)

Leaning on the Everlasting Arms (Elisha A. Hoffman)

Like a River Glorious (Frances Havergal)

Majestic Sweetness Sits Enthroned (Samuel Stennett)

Man of Sorrows! What a Name (Philip P. Bliss)

O for a Heart to Praise My God (Charles Wesley)

O for a Thousand Tongues to Sing (Charles Wesley)

O Love that Wilt Not Let Me Go (George Matheson)

O Sacred Head, Now Wounded (Paul Gerhardt)

O the Deep, Deep Love of Jesus (Samuel T. Francis)

Our Great Savior (J. Wilbur Chapman)

Praise the Savior, Ye Who Know Him (Thomas Kelly)

Rock of Ages (Augustus Toplady)

The God of Abraham Praise (Thomas Olivers)

The Lord's My Shepherd, I'll Not Want (Jessie S. Irvine)

There Is a Fountain Filled with Blood (William Cowper)

This Is My Father's World (Maltbie D. Babcock)

'Tis So Sweet to Trust in Jesus (Louisa M. R. Stead)

Under His Wings (William O. Cushing)

What Wondrous Love Is This (William Walker)

When Morning Gilds the Skies (Edward Caswall)

Heartfelt Thanks

Writing a book on gratitude has served to remind me repeatedly of the enormous debt of thanks I owe to the Lord and to so many others.

I've tried to express my appreciation personally to those who have labored with me to birth this book, but am thankful for the opportunity to acknowledge their contributions publicly:

Lawrence Kimbrough arranged and assembled transcripts of my teaching on gratitude, along with many accumulated resources I unloaded on him, and applied his considerable writing ability to generate the first two drafts of this book.

Lawrence is a humble, gifted servant, and it has been a joy to collaborate with him on this second book. I said it about the last book, and it is true of this one as well: His mark is evident throughout these pages, and it is a better book than I could have written without his help.

Once again, *Greg Thornton* and the devoted staff at Moody Publishers served quietly and capably behind the scenes as this project matured from an embryonic idea into the book you hold in your hands. I have much love and respect for this team of "book midwives"!

Bob Lepine has been a mentor to me and has served on the Advisory Board of Revive Our Hearts since its inception. He helped me think through the message of this book at the outset, and then graciously agreed to provide a theological review of the manuscript. His grasp of Scripture and his skill as a communicator enabled him to provide valuable input and assistance.

Dr. Robert DeMoss, my beloved uncle and friend, reviewed the manuscript and made numerous helpful suggestions.

Under the able, servant-hearted leadership of *Martin Jones*, the entire Revive Our Hearts team willingly shoulders extra demands and responsibilities for prolonged seasons so I can focus on study and writing. These men and women are dearly loved friends and partners in ministry, and I cannot imagine being in the trenches without them.

Mike Neises oversees our ministry publishing efforts with wisdom and grace, and serves as a liaison to our friends at Moody Publishers. My executive assistant, *Sandy Bixel*, covers more bases and handles more tasks on my behalf than anyone will ever know this side of heaven. *Dawn Wilson*, researcher and staff writer for Revive Our Hearts, helped track down a variety of details, illustrations, and sources for this project.

Through their persistent prayers and unflagging encouragement, my dear *"Praying Friends"* provide wind beneath my wings.

"I thank my God in all my remembrance of you . . .
because of your partnership in the gospel from the first day
until now."

Philippians 1:3,5

Notes

Introduction: Your Invitation to Transformation

1. Mary W. Tileston, *Daily Strength for Daily Needs* (New Kensington, PA: Whitaker House, 2003), March 9.

2. Sovereign Grace Ministries Blog, 1/30/09, http://www.sovereigngrace ministries.org/Blog/post/Meet-Wayne-Grudem-(4).aspx.

Chapter 1: The Power of Gratitude

1. Mary Wilder Tileston, *Joy & Strength* (Minneapolis, MN: World Wide Publications, 1986), August 24.

2. Mark Stryker, "Orchestra's Thank-You Notes Strike a Chord with Donor," *The Indianapolis Star*, November 18, 1999, A8.

Chapter 2: Guilt, Grace, and Gratitude

1. Oswald Chambers, *My Utmost for His Highest* (Discovery House; Nashville, TN: Thomas Nelson Publishers) November 20.

2. W. E. Vine, *The Expanded Vine's Expository Dictionary of New Testament Words*, s.v. "thanks."

3. Spiros Zodhiates, *The Complete Word Study New Testament* (Chatanooga, TN: AMG Publishers, 1991), 906.

4. Marvin Olasky, "Thank vs. Thank You," *World* magazine, November 24, 2007.

Chapter 3: No Thanks

1. Elisabeth Elliot, *Keep a Quiet Heart* (Ann Arbor, MI: Servant Publications, 1995), 123.

2. Brandon Baillod, "The Wreck of the Steamer Lady Elgin," Great Lakes Maritime Press, http://www.ship-wreck.com/shipwreck/projects/elgin/. Also see Warren W. Wiersbe, *The Bible Exposition Commentary*, New Testament, vol. 2 (Colorado Springs: Victor, 2001), 114.

3. To sign up for the 30-Day Husband Encouragement Challenge and receive daily emails related to the challenge, go to http://www.reviveourhearts.com/challenge.

4. D. James Kennedy, "The Christian's Magic Wand," printed sermon, Coral Ridge Ministries, November 1996, 7.

5. Paul David Tripp, "Grumbling: A Look at a 'Little' Sin," *The Journal of Biblical Counseling*, vol. 18, no. 2, Winter 2000: 51.

Chapter 4: Why Choose Gratitude?

1. Ellen Vaughn, *Radical Gratitude* (Grand Rapids, MI: Zondervan, 2005), 203.

2. James S. Hewett, *Illustrations Unlimited: A Topical Collection of Hundreds of Stories, Quotations, & Humor for Speakers Writers, Pastors, and Teachers*, ed. (Carol Stream, IL: Tyndale, 1988), 264.

3. Beth Moore, *Breaking Free* (Nashville: B&H Publishing Group, 2003), 71.

Chapter 5: Of Whiners and Worshipers

1. Mary Wilder Tileston, *Joy & Strength* (Minneapolis, MN: World Wide Publications, 1986), August 24.

2. James Baird in a sermon titled, "To Be Thankful," delivered at Independent Presbyterian Church, Savannah, Georgia, October 15, 2006, www.ipcsav.org/resources/sermons/to=be=thankful/.

3. *BreakPoint with Charles Colson*, "Miserable in the Midst of Plenty: The Progress Paradox," August 24, 2004.

4. Steve Dale, "My Pet World," *The Tennessean*, June 29, 2007.

5. *Works of Jonathan Edwards*, volume 2, section VIII: "The Life and Diary of the Rev. David Brainerd with Notes and Reflections," available at Christian Classics Ethereal Library, http://www.ccel.org/ccel/edwards/works2.ix.i.viii.html (book info: http://www.ccel.org/ccel/edwards/works2.html).

6. Matthew Henry, *Matthew Henry's Commentary on the Whole Bible: Complete and Unabridged in One Volume, Regency Reference Library* (Grand Rapids, MI: Zondervan, 1961), Matthew XI.

7. Cited by Dr. Joe McKeever in "Doing the Right Thing Regardless," August 21, 2006, http://www.joemckeever.com/mt/archives/000358.html.

8. Charles Chapman, *Matthew Henry: His Life and Times: A Memorial and a Tribute* (London: Arthur Hall, Virtue & Co., 1859), 114, 116–117, available at Google Books,http://books.google.com/books?q=Matthew+Henry%3A+His+Life+and+Times&btnG=Search+Books.

Chapter 6: How Can I Say Thanks?

1. Olivia Barker, "Whatever Happened to Thank-You Notes?" *USA Today*, December 26, 2005, http://www.usatoday.com/life/lifestyle/2005-12-26-thank-you-notes_x.htm.

2. James S. Hewett, *Illustrations Unlimited: A Topical Collection of Hundreds of Stories, Quotations, & Humor for Speakers Writers, Pastors, and Teachers,* ed. (Carol Stream, IL: Tyndale, 1988), 263.

Chapter 7: Thanks . . . for Everything

1. Charles H. Spurgeon, *Evening by Evening* (Alachua, FL: Bridge-Logos, 2005), December 1.

2. The complete list of "spiritual birthday gifts" is available as a pdf at http://www.reviveourhearts.com/pdf/uploads/45SpiritualGifts.pdf.

3. Illustration by David A. Seamands in the sermon "How to Celebrate Thanksgiving," Preaching Today Tape No. 68, available from www.PreachingTodaySermons.com, a resource of Christianity Today International.

4. "Count Your Blessings," words by Johnson Oatman Jr.

Chapter 8: But Not without Sacrifice

1. Priscilla Maurice, *Sickness, Its Trials and Blessings* (New York: Thomas N. Stanford, 1856), 246.

2. *Life* Magazine, August 1992, 34, 37.

3. Richard Wurmbrand, *In God's Underground* (Bartlesville, OK: Living Sacrifice Book Company, 1968, 2004), 56.

4. Charles H. Spurgeon, Metropolitan Tabernacle Pulpit, "Our Compassionate High Priest," http://www.spurgeon.org/sermons/2251.htm.

5. Glimpses of Christian History, "Congo Rebels Reached Helen Roseveare," August 15, 1964, http://www.christianhistorytimeline.com/DAILYF/2002/08/daily-08-15-2002.shtml.

6. Helen Roseveare, *Living Sacrifice* (Minneapolis, MN: Bethany House, 1979), 20–21.

7. Helen Roseveare, *Digging Ditches* (Geanies House, Fearn, Ross-shire, Scotland: Christian Focus, 2005), 76–77.

8. Elisabeth Elliot, *Suffering Is Not for Nothing*, volume 2, video series (Orlando, FL: Ligonier Ministries, 1989).

Chapter 9: Going Gratitudinal

1. Mary W. Tileston, *Daily Strength for Daily Needs* (New Kensington, PA: Whitaker House, 2003), January 18.

2. Modified from Russell Kelfer, "A Grateful Spirit: Part 2," (176-b), 14, available at http://dtm.org/LessonsOnLine.

3. Anne Keegan, "Blue Christmas," *Chicago Tribune Magazine*, December 24, 1995.

Growing in Gratitude: A 30-Day Devotional Guide

1. Ellen Vaughn, *Radical Gratitude* (Grand Rapids: Zondervan, 2005), 10 (from the foreword by Charles W. Colson).

2. R. J. Morgan, *Nelson's Complete Book of Stories, Illustrations, and Quotes,* electronic ed. (Nashville: Thomas Nelson, 2000), 814.

3. Paul Lee Tan, *Encyclopedia of 7,700 Illustrations* (Rockville, MD: Assurance Publishers, 1979), 1456.

4. R. A. Emmons and M. E. McCullough, "Counting Blessings Versus Burdens: Experimental Studies of Gratitude and Subjective Well-Being in Daily Life," *Journal of Personality and Social Psychology* 84 (2003): 377–89.

5. Nathaniel Philbrick and Thomas Philbrick, eds., *The Mayflower Papers: Selected Writings of Colonial New England* (New York: Penguin Classics, 2007), 34.

6. Edward Winslow, *Good Newes from New England* [1624], ed. Alexander Young (Bedford, MA: Applewood Books, 1996), 54–56.

CHOOSING FORGIVENESS

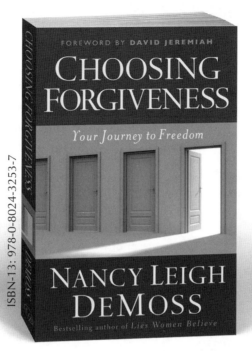

Scripture says that offenses will happen. People will let us down and we will let others down, as well. Forgiveness is left up to us to pray about and then practice. Far from minimizing the hurt of the offense, readers are called to understand that offering forgiveness and letting go of bitterness is the only way to walk in faithfulness. Drawing on biblical teaching of our call to forgive, Nancy shows the reader that forgiveness is a choice–and the only pathway to true freedom. Includes a study guide for individual or group use.

1-800-678-8812 • MOODYPUBLISHERS.COM

LIES WOMEN BELIEVE

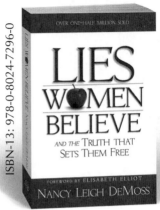

ISBN-13: 978-0-8024-7296-0

We are like Eve. We have all experienced defeats and failures, trouble and turmoil. We have all experienced a selfish heart, a shrewish spirit, anger, envy and bitterness. And we ache to do things over, to have lives of harmony and peace. Nancy Leigh DeMoss exposes those areas of deception most commonly believed by Christian women. She sheds light on how we can be delivered from bondage and set free to walk in God's grace, forgiveness, and abundant life. The book offers the most effective weapon to counter and overcome Satan's deceptions—God's truth.

LIES YOUNG WOMEN BELIEVE

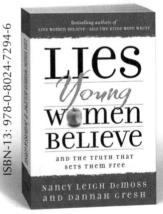

ISBN-13: 978-0-8024-7294-6

The covers of today's teen magazines would make yesteryear's sailor blush. And yet these are the images and messages that teens are flooded with in print and electronic media. *Lies Young Women Believe* will give girls aged 13–19 the tools they need to identify where their lives and beliefs are off course —the result of buying into Satan's lies about God, guys, media, and more. It isn't enough to identify these lies, however. The authors are well-equipped to lead young women in the skills and the truths of Scripture that overcome those lies.

1-800-678-8812 • MOODYPUBLISHERS.COM

Brokenness, Surrender, Holiness

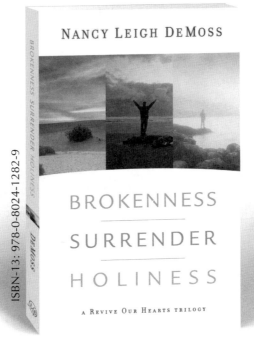

Now the heart-changing volumes can be found in one hardbound and collectible edition. Every great movement of God is preceded by a season of humility and repentance: brokenness. You will never know real joy, peace, or success until you learn what it means to live a fully surrendered life, and have a conscious ambition and aim to be holy. Nancy Leigh DeMoss's life message, with probing questions and application, will be the starting point for giving God the right to revive, control, and purify your heart.

1-800-678-8812 • MOODYPUBLISHERS.COM

Calling Women to Freedom,
Fullness, and Fruitfulness in Christ

Revive Our Hearts™
.com

with Nancy Leigh DeMoss

www.ReviveOurHearts.com